Learn Russian In 7 DAYS!

The Ultimate Crash Course to Learning the Basics of the Russian Language in No Time

By Dagny Taggart

© **Copyright 2015**

All rights reserved. No portion of this book may be reproduced -mechanically, electronically, or by any other means, including photocopying- without the permission of the publisher.

Disclaimer

The information provided in this book is designed to provide helpful information on the subjects discussed. The author's books are only meant to provide the reader with the basics knowledge of a certain language, without any warranties regarding whether the student will, or will not, be able to incorporate and apply all the information provided. Although the writer will make her best effort share her insights, language learning is a difficult task, and each person needs a different timeframe to fully incorporate a new language. This book, nor any of the author's books constitute a promise that the reader will learn a certain language within a certain timeframe.

Table of Contents

MY FREE GIFT TO YOU! 6

LEARN ANY LANGUAGE 300% FASTER 7

    INTRODUCTION: ARE YOU READY FOR AN AMAZING JOURNEY? 8

    CHAPTER 1: ALPHABET AND PRONUNCIATION 11

    CHAPTER 2: GREETINGS AND INTRODUCTIONS (HI, GOOD BYE, HOW ARE YOU?) 22

    CHAPTER 3: WHAT IS AROUND YOU (WHAT, WHERE, WHEN?) 30

    CHAPTER 4: NATIONALITIES AND LANGUAGES 38

    CHAPTER 5: DAYS OF THE WEEK, TELLING THE TIME 43

    CHAPTER 6: TRAVELING AND TRANSPORTATION 51

    CHAPTER 7: ASKING FOR DIRECTIONS (EXCUSE ME, WHERE IS THE...?) 62

    CHAPTER 8: EATING OUT (FOOD + RESTAURANTS) 66

    CHAPTER 9: LET'S GO SHOPPING! 73

    CHAPTER 10: FINDING A PLACE TO STAY 79

    CHAPTER 11: NEAREST AND DEAREST 83

    CHAPTER 12: PERSONALITY (WHAT'S SHE LIKE...?) 89

    CHAPTER 13: PROFESSIONS (TEACHER, LAWYER, SCIENTIST!) 95

    CHAPTER 14: FREE TIME AND HOBBIES 98

    TOP 50 RUSSIAN NOUNS 110

    TOP 50 RUSSIAN VERBS 111

TOP 50 RUSSIAN ADJECTIVES 112

AFTERWORD 114

TIME TO LAUNCH OUT ON YOUR OWN VOYAGE OF DISCOVERY! 114

LEARN ANY LANGUAGE 300% FASTER 115

PS: CAN I ASK YOU A QUICK FAVOR? 116

PREVIEW OF "LEARN SPANISH IN 7 DAYS! - THE ULTIMATE CRASH COURSE TO LEARN THE BASICS OF THE SPANISH LANGUAGE IN NO TIME" 117

CHECK OUT MY OTHER BOOKS 124

ABOUT THE AUTHOR 125

Dedicated to those who love going beyond their own frontiers.

Keep on traveling,

Dagny Taggart

My FREE Gift to You!

As a way of saying thank you for downloading my book, I'd like to send you an exclusive gift that will revolutionize the way you learn new languages. It's an extremely comprehensive PDF with 15 language hacking rules that **will help you learn 300% faster, with less effort, and with higher than ever retention rates**.

This guide is an amazing complement to the book you just got, and could easily be a stand-alone product, but for now I've decided to give it away for free, to thank you for being such an awesome reader, and to make sure I give you all the value that I can to help you succeed faster on your language learning journey.

To get your FREE gift, go to the link below, follow the steps, and I'll send it to your email address right away.

>> http://bitly.com/Language-Gift <<

Learn Any Language 300% FASTER

>> Get Full Online Language Courses With Audio Lessons <<

Would you like to learn a new language? I think that's a great idea. Now, why don't you do it 300% *FASTER*?

I've partnered with the most revolutionary language teachers to bring you the very language online courses I've ever seen. It's a mind-blowing program specifically created for language hackers such as ourselves. It will allow you learn ANY language, from French to Chinese, 3x faster, straight from the comfort of your own home, office, or wherever you may be. It's like having an unfair advantage!

You can choose from a wide variety of languages, such as French, Spanish, Italian, German, Chinese, Portuguese, and A TON more.

Each Online Course consists of:

+ 91 Built-In Lessons
+ 33 Interactive Audio Lessons
+ 24/7 Support to Keep You Going

The program is extremely engaging, fun, and easy-going. You won't even notice you are learning a complex foreign language from scratch. And before you realize it, by the time you go through all the lessons you will officially become a truly solid speaker.

Old classrooms are a thing of the past. It's time for a revolution.

If you'd like to go the extra mile, the click the button below or follow the link, and let the revolution begin

>> http://bitly.com/foreign-language-courses <<

CHECK OUT THE COURSE »

Introduction

Are You Ready For an Amazing Journey?

Hi there! First of all, let me assure you that you are certainly lucky to have this book, because it means that you are about to speak Russian in a short time having so much fun! You are probably the one undaunted in your resolve to start speaking Russian despite all the "bogeyman stories" about people who were beating about in the water of the Russian language, trying not to drown, but in vain… Well, the devil is not as bad as he is painted!

You may need the Russian language because you are just curious about the culture of the Russian people. You are probably tired of those tales about bears walking down the streets and drunken Russians in fur coats playing the balalaika, and you decide to find out how the land lies in reality. You may need some Russian skills because you are in an urgent need of getting on with your colleagues, your boss, your neighbors, and so on… whoever speaking Russian. Or you may be willing to find your destiny from that part of the world. What's so bad about getting in touch with a strikingly beautiful Russian lady or a broad-shouldered good-looking Russian gentleman? It may also be that you are one of those brave personalities, eager to go off on a real journey to this enormous country. And, in this case you definitely need some of the Russian so that you could more or less freely express your thoughts, ideas, and emotions… and tell people how tired you are and how you are missing your home, poor thing (just kidding!). By the way, sometimes the ability to speak the language of the country you are coming to is rewarding, for the reason that you are able not to allow someone to play hanky-panky with you. So, whatever you are, this book is a treasure in your hands.

This Crash Course contains no more than the nitty-gritty that you need to find yourself in the ocean of the Russian language. It's going to be the basis for your "life raft", not yet very firm, but still a vessel able to save your life in the welter of the waves. You are in charge of your raft and you should constantly build it up, so that to make your small boat become a full-fledged ship! So, at that moment you will say: "I speak Russian fluently! I feel absolutely free speaking it! I feel really safe on my ship and, by now, I think there's nothing that I'm not able to put into words!". Have you imagined yourself a captain of such a TITANIC? Good for you, because from this very moment you are on your way to this achievement!

This book is aimed for those who are planning to travel to a Russian-speaking country (such as Russia, Ukraine, Belorussia and other countries of the former USSR) and covers lots of universal communicative situations you may find yourself in, be it doing shopping or looking for some place to spend the night. You are more than welcome to resort to the help of the topic that is the most essential for you at this or that point.

Here are some tips that you may find handy in your journey of learning Russian. Forget your fears. Remember: just go for it, be aggressive, never say die, and you are sure to gain success. So let's get started!

SECTION 1
THE BASICS

Chapter 1: Alphabet and Pronunciation

The Russian alphabet consists of 33 letters, ten of them are vowels, and twenty one of them are consonants. You may wonder what the rest 2 letters are. They are two signs which do not reflect any sounds, but they influence the following sounds. Let's have a look at it:

Letter uppercase /lowercase	Pronunciation of letters in the alphabet	Pronunciation of the letters in the word		Note
		Russian transcription	English transcription	
А / а	а [ah]	а (áрка)	a (father)	
Б / б	бэ [beh]	б (бык)	b (best)	pronounced firmly
В / в	вэ [veh]	в (вóрон)	v (voice)	pronounced firmly
Г / г	гэ [geh]	г (год)	g (great)	pronounced firmly
Д / д	дэ [deh]	д (дочь)	d (drink)	pronounced firmly
Е / е	е [jeh]	е (ель)	je or ye (yet)	
Ё / ё	ё [joh]	ё (ёж)	jo or yo (your)	lips are rounded
Ж / ж	жэ [ʒeh]	ж (жура́вль)	zh (pleasure)	pronounced firmly
З / з	зэ [zeh]	з (знáние)	z (zoo)	pronounced firmly
И / и	и [ee]	и (и́стина)	i (sea)	
Й / й	и крáткое [ee kr'atkoje]	й (йод)	j or y (yes)	
К / к	ка [kah]	к (кот)	k (key)	no aspiration
Л / л	эл [el]	л (Лунá)	l (love)	pronounced firmly
М / м	эм [em]	м (май)	m (milk)	pronounced firmly
Н / н	эн [en]	н (ночь)	n (no)	pronounced firmly
О / о	о [oh]	о (óсень)	o (or)	lips are rounded
П / п	пэ [peh]	п (путь)	p (plan)	pronounced firmly
Р / р	эр [er]	р (роль)	r (right)	pronounced firmly and clearly
С / с	эс [es]	с (сахар)	s (say)	pronounced firmly
Т / т	тэ [teh]	т (три)	t (take)	no aspiration
У / у	у [ooh]	у (у́хо)	u (book)	deep cold sound

Ф / ф	эф [ef]	ф (факт)	f (**f**ace)	pronounced firmly
Х / х	ха [hah]	х (хорошо́)	h (**h**ouse)	pronounced firmly
Ц / ц	цэ [tseh]	ц (царь)	ts (pi**z**za)	pronounced firmly
Ч / ч	чэ [cheh]	ч (чай)	ch (**ch**ance)	
Ш / ш	ша [sha]	ш (шо́рох)	sh (**sh**arp)	pronounced firmly
Щ / щ	ща [shshah]	щ (щека́)	shsh (**sh**eer)	The sound [щ] sounds softer than the sound [ш]
Ъ / ъ (the hard sign)	твёрдый знак [tv'ordyj znak]	--- (подъём)	---	ъ does not have its own pronunciation
Ы / ы	ы [ah]	ы (мысль)	--- (ros**e**s)	sound [ы] sounds like a low sound [и]
Ь / ь (the soft sign)	мягкий знак [my'akkij znak]	--- (лень)	---	ь - does not have its own pronunciation, but makes the preceding sound soft
Э / э	э [eh]	э (э́ра)	e: (m**e**t)	deep sound
Ю / ю	ю [jooh]	ю (юг)	ju or yu (**u**se)	
Я / я	я [jah]	я (янва́рь)	ja or ya (**ya**rd)	

The Word Stress

You've probably noticed **the ́ sign** in some words, such as а́рка, щека́, янва́рь etc. This is a word stress mark. Stress is essential for words consisting of more than one syllable. Consider that it is not normally printed in Russian written texts. However, these signs are necessary for language learners to find out how to pronounce the words without messing up their meanings! Sometimes it's really curious how the meanings of some words change depending on the stress:

> **За́мок** = a castle; **замо́к** = a lock.
> **Му́ка** = pain, suffering; **мука́** = flour.

As you can see, the meanings of similar words with different word stress are absolutely diverse, so look out and focus your attention on the stress when you learn new words.

NOTE: Stress in Russian isn't fixed, except one case: a syllable with **ё** is always stressed, so we don't put the stress mark above it.

Vowel and Consonant Systems

Now let's have a closer look at the systems of vowel and consonant sounds. Some good news for you: there are some sounds like [б], [в], [м], [с], [з] which are almost the same as the English [b], [v], [m], [s], [z]. There are also some sounds that have a slight difference in the way we pronounce them, such as [д], [т], [р], [х], [н]; here are their English counterparts [d], [t], [r], [h], [n]. And, of course, there are some sounds in Russian that are missing in the English sound system, e.g. [щ], [ц] and soft sounds. Therefore you'll be definitely surprised at the fact that many consonants are basically firm, but they have their soft counterparts, for example: [д]- [д'], [т]- [т'], [р]- [р']. These soft sounds are palatalized, i.e. they are produced by the tongue positioned near the palate. As a matter of fact, you'll need some time and effort to utter all these sounds properly. So warm up a little bit and get ready for new sounds to come off your lips! Remember the proverb: you must spoil before you spin!

Vowel Sounds

Let's observe the vowel system in detail. Pay attention to the fact that vowels behave differently depending on:

- **Stressed/unstressed position** of the syllable containing the vowel
- The position of the vowel inside the word: in the **beginning** of a word and after **ь** and **ъ** / in the **middle** and at the **end** of a word

Vowel	How to pronounce it in a word	The quality of the sound in certain cases:	Russian word + its meaning:
а	[ah] only a stressed sound is more intense than an unstressed one	Stressed: <u>au</u>nt	мама (mom)

я	[j] + [ah]	The beginning of the word and after ь and ъ: **y**ard	я́блоко (apple) пья́ный (tipsy)
	[ah]	The middle and the end of the word: m**u**st	дятел (woodpecker)
о	[oh]	Stressed: lips are rounded - between r**o**le and t**a**lk	кот (cat)
	[ah]	Unstressed: m**u**st	Москва́ (Moscow)
ё	[j] + [oh] lips are rounded	The beginning of the word and after ь and ъ: **Yo**rk	ёлка (pine tree) шьёт (he/she is sewing)
	[oh]	The middle and the end of the word: between r**o**le and t**a**lk	мёд (honey)
э	[eh] only a stressed sound is more intense than an unstressed one	Stressed: between **e**gg and c**a**t	Мэри (Mary)
		Unstressed: a neutral sound - **a**bout	эле́ктрик (electrician)
е	[j] + [eh]	The beginning of the word and after ь and ъ: **ye**sterday	ехать (to go by transport)
	[eh]	The middle and the end of the word: **a**bout	река (river)
у	lips are rounded and	As in z**oo**, but the sound is more intense	Владимир Путин

	stretched-out as if you are kissing the air!		(Vladimir Putin) улыбка (a smile)
ю	[j] + [uh] lips are rounded and stretched-out	The beginning of the word and after ь and ъ: comp**u**ter	Юг (south) пью (I drink)
	[uh]	The middle and the end of the word: b**oo**k	любовь (love)
и	[ee] a stressed sound is more intense than an unstressed one	As in d**ee**p, but shorter in length	мир (world, peace) ноги (legs)
ы	[i] an unusual, deep sound, sometimes they say that you should pronounce it as if you've been punched in the stomach!	The sound between ar**ou**nd and m**e**.	ты (you) мы (we) мыло (soap) торты (cakes)

You might have noticed that the vowels were presented in the following order: [a]-[*я*]; [o]-[*ё*]; [э]-[*e*]; [y]-[*ю*] and [ы]-[*u*]. These are hard/*soft* pairs. All the soft vowel sounds (in italics) soften or palatalize the preceding consonant regardless of their position (stressed or unstressed, at the beginning or in the middle of the word etc.).

Let's take some suitable examples from the table above (the soft consonants are underlined):

Д̲я̲тел - [д'], [т']; мёд - [м']; э̲л̲ектр̲и̲к [л'], [р']; р̲ека - [р']; ног̲и - [г'], м̲ир [м'].

15

Consonant Sounds

Group 1

Let's take a good look at the consonant system. Try to guess according to what principle this group appears here:

Consonant	How to pronounce it in a word	As in…	Russian word + its meaning:
б	similar to English [b]	boy	ба́бушка (granny)
	At the end of the word and before voiceless consonants: similar to English [p], but without aspiration	play	хле́б [хлеп] (bread)
п	similar to English [p], but without aspiration	play	па́па (dad)
в	similar to English [v]	very	волк (wolf)
	At the end of the word and before voiceless consonants: similar to English [f]	fast	рыболо́в [рыбало́ф] (fisher)
ф	similar to English [f]	fast	фле́йта (flute)
г	similar to English [g]	greek	год (year)
	At the end of the word and before voiceless consonants: similar to English [k], but no aspiration is made	skate	утю́г [утю́к] (an iron)
к	similar to English [k], but no aspiration is made	skate	ке́пка (cap)
д	similar to English [d], but with tongue against upper teeth	date	Да́ша (Dasha – Russian name)

	At the end of the word and before voiceless consonants: similar to English [t], but no aspiration is made	take	сад [сат] (garden) лодка [лотка] (boat)
т	similar to English [t], but with tongue against upper teeth and no aspiration is made	take	Táня (Tanya – Russian name)
	similar to the sound [ʒ]	measure	жáрко (it's hot)
ж	At the end of the word and before voiceless consonants: similar to English [ʃ], but with the tip of the tongue further back in the mouth	sure	нож [нош] (knife) ложка [лошка] (spoon)
ш	similar to English [ʃ], but with the tip of the tongue further back in the mouth	sure	шýба (fur coat)
	similar to English [z]	zebra	звездá (a star)
з	At the end of the word and before voiceless consonants: similar to English [s]	snake	блюз [блюс] (blues)
с	similar to English [s]	snake	óстров (island)

Have you guessed right? These were pairs of voiced/*voiceless* consonant sounds [б]-[*п*]; [в]-[*ф*]; [г]-[*к*]; [д]-[*т*]; [ж]-[*ш*] and [з]-[*с*]. Remember that all voiced sounds become voiceless at the end of the word. Imagine that you get too tired to use your voice by the time you reach the end of the word, and utter its voiceless counterpart. The voiced sounds also become voiceless before other voiceless sounds. It seems to be contagious! Let's take some examples from the table above:

Хлеб [хлеп] – the voiced [б] becomes the voiceless [п] at the end of the word;

нож [нош] - the voiced [ж] becomes the voiceless [ш] at the end of the word;

лодка [лотка] - the voiced [д] becomes the voiceless [т] before the voiceless [к].

These consonants, except [ж]-[ш], may also be influenced by soft vowels, which we mentioned in the previous chapter. Practice to pronounce these palatalized sounds:
[б']-[п']; [в']-[ф']; [г']-[к']; [д']-[т']; [з']-[с'].

Practice reading these words. The soft vowel sounds are underlined; the soft consonant sounds are in bold:

берёза (birch)
Петербург (St. Petersburg)
ветер (wind)
фигура (figure)
Геркулес (Hercules)
киви (kiwi)
дядя (uncle)
тётя (aunt)
Земля (Earth)
сестра (sister)

Group 2

Take a look at another group of consonants. What do you think their common feature is?

Consonant	How to pronounce it in a word	As in...	Russian word + its meaning:
л	similar to English [l]	luck	ла́мпа (lamp)
м	similar to English [m]	mother	май (May)
н	similar to English [n], but with tongue against upper teeth	Montreal	нос (nose)
р	similar to English [r], but you should produce intense vibration of your tongue at the roof of your mouth	rabbit	ро́бот (robot)

й	similar to English [j]; it's also a part of some vowel sounds	**y**acht	**й**о́га (yoga) сто**й** (stop)

You were right if you had supposed that the sounds in the table above are sonorants! Such sounds are always voiced and are very clear, resonant by nature. The sound [й] is even considered a semi-vowel! Do you remember what vowel sounds contain [j]? These are [я], [е], [ё], [ю].

All sonorants except [й] are palatalized under the influence of soft vowels. Practice the pronunciation of palatalized sounds:

[л']; [м']; [н']; [р'].

Practice reading these words. The soft vowel sounds are underlined; the soft consonant sounds are in bold:

ли́мон (lemon)
по́**л**е (field)
мя́со (meat)
и́**м**я (name)
ня́**н**я (nanny)
не**д**е́**л**я (week)
Рим (Rome)
Бо́**р**я (Borya - Russian male name)

Group 3

In this table you are going to discover all the rest consonants of the Russian language.

Consonant	How to pronounce it in a word	As in…	Russian word + its meaning:
х	similar to English [h], but more intense	**h**ot	**х**о́лодно (It's cold)
ц	similar to English [ts]	piz**z**a	**ц**ентр (downtown, center)

ч	similar to English [tʃ]	**ch**air	человек (a person, a human being)
щ	similar to the English [ʃ]; softer than Russian [ш], the tongue is farther forward	Spani**sh sh**irt	щи (shchi – Russian cabbage soup)

Only the sound [x] can be influenced by soft vowels. In this case it becomes [x']. Try to pronounce it.

Now read these words palatalizing the [x] sound:

хи́трый (sly)

хи́-**х**и́ (he,he – laughing sound)

с**х**е́ма (scheme)

Group 4 (Signs)

All right, we're almost there! What are those mysterious the soft and the hard sign? Have a look at the table:

Sign	How to say the letter	Function in a word	Russian word + its meaning:
ъ (rarely used)	твёрдый знак tv'ordyj znak	indicates the [j] sound between a consonant and a vowel	подъём [pad'jom] (getting up)
ь (often used, especially at the end of a word)	мягкий знак m'akkij znak	makes the preceding sound soft	день (day)
		indicates the [j] sound between a consonant and a vowel	воробьи [varab'ji] (sparrows)

Practice reading these words. Then answer 3 questions about them.

The soft vowel sounds are underlined; the soft consonant sounds are in bold:

конь (male horse)
мать (mother)
Нью-Йорк (New York)
Илья (Ilya – Russian name)
июнь (June)
дочь (daughter)
ночь (night)
мощь (power)

1. In which words the soft sign makes the preceding sound palatalized?

2. In which words it indicates the [j] sound between a consonant and a vowel?

3. And in which words it has no influence at all? Why?

Answer:

1. Конь, мать, июнь.
2. Нью-Йорк, Илья.
3. Дочь, ночь, мощь. The sounds [ч] and [щ] cannot be palatalized.

Congratulations! You have just completed a mini-course on Russian phonetics! By this moment you should be able to read in Russian, but still, if you're not sure how to pronounce a word, you can always use *Google translate:* type a word and click on the speaker icon in the bottom left corner to hear the approximate pronunciation. Be careful though! Those are not done by Native Russian speakers. The best way to get the hang of the Russian phonetics is to listen and imitate real speech. So try to watch movies in Russian and communicate with Native speakers as much as possible.

Chapter 2: Greetings and Introductions (Hi, Good Bye, How Are You?)

Приве́т! Как дела́?

First of all, let's learn how to call people around you:

I	я
You (singular)	ты
You (plural, polite)	вы
He	он
She	она́
It (neuter)	оно́
We	мы
They	они́

There are no equivalents of personal titles like Mr, Mrs etc. in the Russian-speaking world. If you address a stranger or, for example, your professor or an elderly person, you should use the polite form **вы** instead of **ты** (which is actually a plural form of it). Sometimes the polite form (Вы) is capitalized in formal documents, official invitations etc. If you are not sure which form to choose in everyday life - just go with **вы** to be on the safe side. Your conversation partner can always say: "Дава́й на «ты»!". (Let's call each other **ты**). It means that the air between you has got more relaxed and you can address him or her "**ты**".

Here is a list of common greetings in Russian.

Common Greetings

Hi	Приве́т
Hello	Здра́вствуйте
Good Morning	До́брое у́тро
Good Afternoon	До́брый день
Good evening	До́брый ве́чер
Good night (before going to sleep)	Споко́йной но́чи

Asking and Answering 'How are you?'

Are you good at saying «Здравствуйте» and «Спокойной ночи»? If so, it's high time to discover some common expressions like «Как дела?».

How are you? (informal)	Как дела?
How are you? (formal)	Как у вас делá?
How are you doing? (informal)	Как (ты) поживáешь?
How are you doing? (formal)	Как (вы) поживáете?
Well/Very well	Хорошó/Óчень хорошó
Good and you? (informal)	Хорошó, а у тебя́?
Good and you? (formal)	Хорошó, а у вас?
So-so	Тáк себе
What's up? What's new?	Какúе нóвости?

Practice saying **Привет! Как дела?** to your friends! Have fun, and you are sure to learn faster!

Saying Goodbye

These are common expressions that we say parting from someone.

Goodbye (informal)	Покá
Goodbye (formal)	До свидáния
See you later	До скóрого
See you tomorrow	До зáвтра
See you	Увúдимся

And don't forget to express your gratitude before you go by saying the magic word *Спасибо!* (Thank you!)

Show Your Performance!

Translate the following conversation into English

#1

A: Дóбрый день, Áнна!
B: Привéт, Антóн!
A: Как дела?
B: Очень хорошó, а у тебя́?
A: Тáк себе.
B: Покá, Антóн!

A: Увидимся, Анна!

Introductions and Other phrases

One of the frequently asked questions that language learners stumble upon all the time is certainly Как тебя зовут? (What is your name?). By the way, the simplest way to answer this question is to say e.g. Я Наташа (I'm Natasha). Practice saying: <u>Я + your name.</u>

What is your name? (informal)	Как тебя зовут?
What is your name? (formal)	Как вас зовут?
My name is...	Меня зовут...
Nice to meet you!	Приятно познако́миться!
It's a pleasure.	Очень приятно.
Me too.	Мне тоже.
How old are you?	Ско́лько тебе́ лет? (informal)
I'm ... years old.	Ско́лько вам лет? (formal)

It's noteworthy that the verb endings ТСЯ, ТЬСЯ always sound like [tsa]-[ца], like in the word царь (tsar). E.g. Приятно познако́ми**ться**! [познакомица].

There is a running joke among Russians. They say: Приятно познакомиться, царь. (Nice to meet you, I'm a tsar). Try to say it with a serious face. It'll definitely surprise your conversation partners!

Other Useful Phrases

When people speak a foreign language it's very natural if they don't understand some words or phrases. As a result they may want to ask to speak slower or to request some explanations.

I don't understand.	Я не понима́ю.
Can you repeat, please? (plural and formal)	(Вы) мо́жете повтори́ть, пожа́луйста?
Speak more slowly, please. (plural and formal)	Говори́те ме́дленнее, пожа́луйста.
How do you say ...?	Как сказа́ть ...?
What does this mean?	Что э́то зна́чит?
What is this?	Что э́то?
Can you help me? (plural and formal)	Вы мо́жете помо́чь мне?

Do you speak English? (plural and formal)	Вы говори́те по-англи́йски?
I speak a little Spanish.	Я немно́го говорю́ по-ру́сски.
I don't know.	(Я) не зна́ю.
Write it down, please.	Напиши́те э́то, пожа́луйста.

Here we are coming across the negative particle НЕ (pronounced [н'э]).

E.g. Я <u>не</u> понима́ю. = I do<u>n't</u> understand.

Consequently, you can attach the opposite meaning to this sentence by omitting the word НЕ:

E.g. Я понима́ю. = I understand.

Do you feel that something's missing? Oh, yes! Another good thing about Russian is that there are NO articles and linking verbs! So, we don't have to use DO, DOES, AM, IS, ARE etc. in negations and questions. Let's take a couple of sentences from above as an example:

What *is* this? (3 words) = Что э́то? (2 words):
What = Что; this = э́то.
What *does* this mean? (4 words) = Что э́то зна́чит? (3 words):
What = Что, this = э́то, mean = зна́чит.

Show Your Performance!

Translate the following conversation into English

#2

A: До́брый ве́чер!

B: Здра́вствуйте! Как вы пожива́ете?

A: Хорошо́, а вы?

B: Очень хорошо́, спаси́бо.

A: Как вас зову́т?

B: Меня зовут Роман. А как вас зовут?

A: Я Елена.

B: Сколько вам лет, Елена?

A: Мне 25 лет. А вам?

B: Мне 27 лет. Откуда вы?

A: Я из Петербурга, а вы?

B: А я из Сочи.

A: Очень приятно!

B: Мне тоже очень приятно.

Match the phrase in English with the corresponding phrase in Russian:

1.	I don't understand.	a.	(Я) не знаю.
2.	Can you repeat, please? (plural and formal)	b.	Что это?
3.	Speak more slowly, please. (plural and formal)	c.	Напишите это, пожалуйста.
4.	How do you say …?	d.	Вы говорите по-английски?
5.	What does this mean?	e.	Как сказать …?
6.	What is this?	f.	Что это значит?
7.	Can you help me? (plural and formal)	g.	(Вы) можете повторить, пожалуйста?
8.	Do you speak English? (plural and formal)	h.	Вы можете помочь мне?
9.	I speak a little Russian.	i.	Я немного говорю по-русски.
10.	I don't know.	j.	Говорите медленнее, пожалуйста.
11.	Write it down, please.	k.	Я не понимаю.

Chapter 2: Check Yourself

Translation #1

A: Добрый день, Анна!

B: Привет, Антон!

A: Как дела?

B: Очень хорошо, а у тебя?

A: Та́к себе́.

B: Пока, Антон!

A: Увидимся, Анна!

A: Good afternoon Anna!

B: Hi Anton!

A: How are you?

B: Very well, and you?

A: So-so.

B: Bye, Anton!

A: See you, Anna!

Translation #2

A: Добрый вечер!

B: Здравствуйте! Как вы поживаете?

A: Хорошо, а вы?

B: Очень хорошо, спасибо.

A: Как вас зовут?

B: Меня зовут Роман. А как вас зовут?

A: Я Елена.

B: Сколько вам лет, Елена?

A: Мне 25 лет. А вам?

B: Мне 27 лет. Откуда вы?

A: Я из Петербурга, а вы?

B: А я из Сочи.

A: Очень приятно!

B: Мне тоже очень приятно.

A: Good evening!

B: Hello! How are you? (formal)

A: I'm well, and you?

B: Very well, thank you.

A: What's your name? (formal)

B: My name's Roman. And what is your name?

A: I'm Elena.

B: How old are you, Elena?

A: I'm 25 years old. And you?

B: I'm 27 years old. Where are you from?

A: I'm from St. Petersburg, and you?

B: I'm from Sochi.

A: Nice to meet you!

B: It's a pleasure for me too!

Match the phrase in English with the corresponding phrase in Russian:

1.	I don't understand.	k.	Я не понима́ю.
2.	Can you repeat, please? (plural and formal)	g.	(Вы) мо́жете повтори́ть, пожа́луйста?
3.	Speak more slowly, please. (plural and formal)	j.	Говори́те ме́дленнее, пожа́луйста.
4.	How do you say …?	e.	Как сказа́ть …?
5.	What does this mean?	f.	Что э́то зна́чит?
6.	What is this?	b.	Что э́то?
7.	Can you help me? (plural and formal)	h.	Вы мо́жете помо́чь мне?
8.	Do you speak English? (plural and formal)	d.	Вы говори́те по-англи́йски?
9.	I speak a little Spanish.	i.	Я немно́го говорю́ по-ру́сски.
10.	I don't know.	a.	(Я) не зна́ю.
11.	Write it down, please.	c.	Напиши́те э́то, пожа́луйста.

Chapter 3: What Is Around You (What, Where, When?)

As a child, you used to be constantly exploring the world. Every new day was a miracle and brought a new range of fresh impressions and bright emotions. You were getting to know rules and principles of your Native language in a natural and simple way, and, what is more, it happened subconsciously! It's great for you to know, because it may help you to perceive Russian as a foreign language more easily! Many psychologists recommend attaching emotions, sensations and associations to the learning process. That's why when you get acquainted with some new words or language phenomena you should look, listen, draw and/or touch as many things as possible, communicate as much as possible, find as many funny/curious things as possible, so that the moment of your touching/drawing a thing or when you are laughing, you are creating an association in your brain that is going to help you to extract this knowledge from the depths of your mind. We strongly recommend that you practice saying new words and expressions with your friends, or employ them in a conversation with a Native speaker.

Here are the basic question words that you need to ask lots of questions.

Question Words

What?	Что? [што]
Where?	Где?
When?	Когда́?
Who?	Кто́?
Why?	Почему́?
Which?	Кото́рый?

You should learn the basic question *Что это?* (What's this?). If you change the first word in this question to Кто́? you'll get *Кто это?* (Who's this?). By the way, you can say *Это что? Это кто?* as well.

The word order in Russian is not fixed, but there is a scheme which is considered basic: the Subject + the Verb + the Object. Let's show it on the illustrious phrase **I love you.**

<u>Subject + Verb + Object:</u> You can say *Я люблю тебя*, and it will sound neutral.

<u>Subject + Object + Verb:</u> You can as well say *Я тебя люблю*, and it will mean absolutely the same.

<u>Verb + Subject + Object:</u> If you say *Люблю я тебя!* it will sound more emphatic: *Yes, I do love you*, as if you were asked many times if you do or not. In this case, the sentence stress is on the Verb.

<u>Object + Subject + Verb:</u> If you say *Тебя я люблю!*, you ascertain that you love not Natasha, not Dasha... but exactly the person you are saying it to. In this case, the sentence stress is on the Object.

This is ... (about a thing or a person) = Это ...

Show Your Performance!

Read aloud, guess the meaning of the new words, and translate the following phrases into English

1. - Что э́то? – Это компью́тер.
2. - Кто э́то? – Это Ма́ша.
3. - Что э́то? – Это телефо́н.
4. - Кто э́то? – Это ба́бушка.
5. – Это что? – Это ма́ска.
6. – Это кто? – Это ба́йкер.
7. – Это что? – Это конте́йнер.
8. – Это кто? – Это пило́т.

Match the question words in English with their Russian equivalents:

1. What?	a. Когда́?
2. Where?	b. Кто?
3. When?	c. Почему́?
4. Who?	d. Кото́рый?
5. Why?	e. Где?
6. Which?	f. Что?

This is a "survival kit" – the most essential words for basic needs:

Useful words and phrases

Yes	Да
No	Нет
But	Но
Also/too	То́же
And	И
Or	Или
Now	Сейча́с
Well	Ну…
Sorry	Извини́те
Excuse me	Прости́те
Thank you	Спаси́бо
You're welcome	Не за что
Please	Пожа́луйста
Me too.	Я то́же
Very	Очень
A lot	Мно́го
That's okay/Okay	Всё хорошо́

You also have to be able to count so that to talk about the age, to deal with money etc.

Numbers 1-10

1	оди́н
2	два
3	три
4	четы́ре
5	пять
6	шесть
7	семь
8	во́семь
9	де́вять
10	де́сять

Numbers 11-20

11	оди́ннадцать
12	двена́дцать

13	трина́дцать
14	четы́рнадцать
15	пятна́дцать
16	шестна́дцать
17	семна́дцать
18	восемна́дцать
19	девятна́дцать
20	два́дцать

Note: All numbers from 11 to 19 have the **надцать** component. There is a corresponding 1-9 number in the same (<u>один</u>надцать) or a bit different (<u>две</u>надцать) form that precedes the ending **надцать**.

The pattern for the numbers 21-29: <u>двадцать</u> + <u>a number</u> as two separate words.

E.g. 21 ---> два́дцать оди́н, 22 ---> двадцать два, 23 ---> двадцать три, etc.

Numbers 30-100+

30	три́дцать
40	сорок
50	пятьдеся́т
60	шестьдеся́т
70	се́мьдесят
80	во́семьдесят
90	девяно́сто
100	сто
105	сто пять
115	сто пятна́дцать

- The pattern for the numbers 31-99: тридцать + a number as two separate words. There are NO hyphens, NO "и" (and).

E.g. 33 = тридцать один; 45 = сорок пять; 78 = семьдесят восемь
- The pattern for the numbers 31-99: сто + the number

E.g. 190 = сто девяносто (see above)

- Look out! If you say соро́к instead of со́рок, you will be misunderstood, because соро́к means *of magpies* (it's a kind of bird). You don't want other people start looking around and ask you: Где? (Where?).

Learn to talk about the age:

How old are you? (informal)	Ско́лько тебе́ лет?
How old are you? (plural, formal)	Ско́лько вам лет?
I am… years old.	Мне… лет.
How old is Masha? Masha is … years old.	Ско́лько Ма́ш<u>е</u> … лет? Ма́ш<u>е</u> … лет.
How old is Roma? Roma is … years old.	Ско́лько Ро́м<u>е</u> … лет? Ро́м<u>е</u> … лет.

Note: Pay attention to the change of endings in the names. It happens in accordance with the Case of the Noun, in this example it's the **dative case** showing that that something is given or addressed to the person.

Show Your Performance!

Read aloud, guess the meaning of the new words, and translate the following phrases into English

1. – Ско́лько тебе́ лет? - Мне 22 го́да.
2. – Ско́лько вам лет? - Мне 75 лет.
3. – Ско́лько Анато́лию лет? - Анато́лию 30 лет.
4. – Ско́лько Еле́не лет? - Еле́не 46 лет.
5. – Ско́лько Алексе́ю лет? - Алексе́ю 57 лет.
6. – Ско́лько ребёнку лет? - Ребёнку 9 лет. (ребенок = child).

Numbers 200-1000

200	две́сти
300	три́ста
400	четы́реста
500	пятьсо́т
600	шестьсо́т
700	семьсо́т
800	восемьсо́т
900	девятьсо́т
1000	ты́сяча

10000	де́сять ты́сяч
1000000	миллио́н

The principle is the same: NO hyphens, NO "и" (and). You just start with the biggest figure and finish with the smallest. Let's take a complex number:
1200345 = миллион двести тысяч триста сорок пять

Show Your Performance!

Practice saying these numbers in Russian:

160, 346, 574, 621, 735, 812, 999, 1200, 1570, 2404, 5340, 12444, 38826, 1435972

Colors

Red	кра́сный (-ая), (-ое)
Orange	ора́нжевый (-ая), (-ое)
Yellow	жёлтый (-ая), (-ое)
Green	зелёный (-ая), (-ое)
Blue	си́ний (-яя), (-ее)
Light blue	голубо́й (-ая), (-ое)
Pink	ро́зовый (-ая), (-ое)
Black	чёрный (-ая), (-ое)
White	бе́лый (-ая), (-ое)
Brown	кори́чневый (-ая), (-ое)
Gray	се́рый (-ая), (-ое)
Light	све́тлый (-ая), (-ое)
Dark	тёмный (-ая), (-ое)

Note how the endings are changed in the feminine and neutral forms. Another important feature of the Russian language - Adjective and Noun Agreement. Russian adjectives agree with nouns in gender (feminine, masculine or neutral), case and number (singular or plural). For example, blue pencils (m., pl.) (си́ние карандаши́); black male cat (m., sing.) (чёрный кот); warm weather (f., sing.) (тёплая пого́да).

Let's take some basic objects that you come across every day:

handbag	су́мка *f*

apple	я́блоко n
tree	де́рево n
pen	ру́чка f
flower	цвето́к m
bird	пти́ца f
book	кни́га f
chocolate	шокола́д m
chair	стул m
table	стол m
door	дверь f
street	у́лица f
car	маши́на f

Show Your Performance!

Make up the following phrases paying attention to the gender agreement.

A red car, a black cat, a blue pen, dark chocolate, a white bird, an orange book, a yellow table, a green tree, a light blue handbag, a pink flower, a brown chair, a gray door, a light street.

Chapter 3: Check Yourself

Read aloud, guess the meaning of the new words, and translate the following phrases into English

1. – What's this? – It's a computer.
2. - Who's this? – It's Masha.
3. - What's this – It's a phone.
4. - Who's this? – It's a granny.
5. – What's this? – It's a mask.
6. – Who's this? – It's biker.
7. – What's this? – It's a container.
8. – Who's this? – It's a pilot.

Match the question words in English with their Russian equivalents:

1. What?	f. Что?
2. Where?	e. Где?
3. When?	a. Когда́?
4. Who?	b. Кто?

5.	Why?	c. Почему́?
6.	Which?	d. Кото́рый?

Read aloud, guess the meaning of the new words, and translate the following phrases into English

1. – How old are you? – I'm 22.
2. – How old are you? – I'm 75.
3. – How old is Anatoly? – Anatoly's 30.
4. – How old is Elena? – Elena's 46.
5. – How old is Alexey? – Alexey's 57.
6. – How old is the child? – The child is 9.

Practice saying these numbers in Russian:

160 – сто шестьдеся́т, 346 – три́ста со́рок шесть, 574 – пятьсо́т се́мьдесят четы́ре, 621 – шестьсо́т два́дцать оди́н, 735 – семьсо́т три́дцать пять, 812 – восемьсо́т двена́дцать, 999 – девятьсо́т девяно́сто де́вять, 1200 – ты́сяча две́сти, 1570 - ты́сяча пятьсо́т се́мьдесят, 2404 – две ты́сячи четы́реста четы́ре, 5340 – пять ты́сяч три́ста со́рок, 12444 – двена́дцать ты́сяч четы́реста со́рок четы́ре, 38826 три́дцать во́семь ты́сяч восемьсо́т два́дцать шесть, 1435972 – миллио́н четы́реста три́дцать пять ты́сяч девятьсо́т се́мьдесят два

Make up the following phrases paying attention to the gender agreement.

Кра́сная маши́на, чёрная ко́шка, си́няя ру́чка, тёмный шокола́д, бе́лая пти́ца, ора́нжевая кни́га, жёлтый стол, зелёное де́рево, голуба́я су́мка, ро́зовый цвето́к, кори́чневый стул, се́рая дверь, све́тлая у́лица.

Chapter 4: Nationalities and Languages

Откуда ты?

What's one of the most common questions for a traveler and a language learner you have to be able to ask and answer? Sure, *Откуда ты?* (Where are you from?).

First of all, let's go over the word WHERE and its 3 connotations in Russian:

> Where at? = где?
> Where to? = куда́?
> Where from? = отку́да?

As you have probably guessed, in this chapter we are interested in the last one – *отку́да?*

Now read the Russian title of this chapter. Very simple, isn't it? Two words - *Отку́да ты?* It is an informal way to ask *Where are you from?*

To answer this question, you say

> Я из + the name of the country in the <u>genitive</u> case.

The genitive case suggests the idea that something (somebody) belongs or refers to something (somebody). Its meaning in English is equivalent to the one of the preposition **of**.

Here are the expressions that can help you to find out where your conversation partner is from and to say where you are from. The genitive case of the countries is given in bold (the stress does not change).

Where are you from? (informal)	Отку́да ты?
Where are you from? (formal, plural)	Отку́да вы?
I am from …	Я из …
The USA	США [сша] (**США**)
The UK	Великобрита́ния (**Великобрита́нии**)
Australia	Австра́лия (**Австра́лии**)
Canada	Кана́да (**Кана́ды**)
Brazil	Брази́лия (**Брази́лии**)

Argentina	Аргенти́на (**Аргенти́ны**)
France	Фра́нция (**Фра́нции**)
Spain	Испа́ния (**Испа́нии**)
Russia	Росси́я (**Росси́и**)

Show Your Performance!

Match the phrases in English with their Russian equivalents:

1. Where are you from? (informal)	a. Ты говоришь по-русски?
2. Where are you from? (formal, plural)	b. Я из …
3. I am from …	c. Вы говорите по-русски?
4. Do you speak Russian? (informal)	d. Откуда вы?
5. Do you speak Russian? (formal, plural)	e. Откуда ты?

Read aloud, guess the meaning of the new words, and translate the following phrases into English:

1. - Отку́да ты? - Я из Брази́лии.
2. - Отку́да вы? - Я из Кана́ды.
3. – Отку́да она́? – Она́ из Фра́нции.
4. – Отку́да они́? – Они́ из Аргенти́ны.
5. – Отку́да он? – Он из Гре́ции.
6. - Отку́да ты? – Я из США.
7. – Отку́да он? – Он из Герма́нии.

Now it's time to talk about nationalities. The structure of a sentence like *I'm American* is ridiculously simple! You just say Я… and add a nationality. Find your nationality in the list below (female gender is given in bold):

I'm …	Я…
American	америка́нец (америка́н**ка**)
English	англича́нин (англича́н**ка**)
Australian	австрали́ец (австрали́й**ка**)
Canadian	кана́дец (кана́д**ка**)
Brazilian	брази́лец (бразилья́н**ка**)
Argentinian	аргенти́нец (аргенти́н**ка**)

French	француз (француженка)
Spansih	испанец (испанка)
Russian	русский (русская)

Note: male nationalities end with **–ец, -ин**, etc. but female nationalities nearly always end with **–ка.**

Make sure you know the phrase *Do you speak English?* before you go to Russia or a Russian-speaking country. You'll probably feel relieved to find out that many people actually speak English.

| Do you speak English? (informal) | Ты говоришь по-английски? |
| Do you speak English? (formal, plural) | Вы говорите по-английски? |

Get ready to express your reaction in a dialogue, here come some emotional exclamations!

Cool!	Класс! (Классно!)
Great!	Здорово!
How interesting!	Как интересно!

Show Your Performance!

Translate into English:

A: Здравствуйте! Вы говорите по-английски?
B: Добрый день, нет. Вы англичанин?
A: Нет, я из Австралии. Я австралиец.
B: Здорово! Моя бабушка австралийка. А как вас зовут?
A: Меня зовут Томас. А как вас зовут?
B: Я Алиса.
A: Очень приятно!
B: Мне тоже. Ну, пока!
A: До свидания!

Put the words in the table according to their gender:

машина	кошка	ручка	испанец	бразильянка	птица
кот		англичанин	книга	американка	стол
француз		дерево	итальянец	сумка	цветок
канадец	стул	дверь	улица		

| Он американец, … |
| Она студентка, … |
| Оно окно, … |

Chapter 4: Check Yourself

Match the phrases in English with their Russian equivalents:

1. Where are you from? (informal)	e. Откуда ты?
2. Where are you from? (formal, plural)	d. Откуда вы?
3. I am from …	b. Я из …
4. Do you speak Russian? (informal)	a. Ты говоришь по-русски?
5. Do you speak Russian? (formal, plural)	c. Вы говорите по-русски?

Read aloud, guess the meaning of the new words, and translate the following phrases into English:

1. - Where are you from? - I'm from Brazil.
2. - Where are you from? - I'm from Canada.
3. - Where is she? - She's from France.
4. - Where are they? - They are from Argentina.
5. - Where is he? - He's from Greece.
6. - Where are you from? - I am from the USA.
7. - Where is he? - He's from Germany.

Translate into English:

A: Hello! Do you speak English?
B: Good afternoon, no. Are you English?
A: No, I'm from Australia. I am Australian.
B: Great! My granny is Australian. What's your name?
A: My name is Thomas. What's your name?
B: I'm Alice.
A: It's a pleasure!
B: To me too. Well, bye!
A: Goodbye!

Put the words in the table according to their gender:

Он американец, испанец, кот, англичанин, стол, француз, итальянец, цветок, канадец, стул
Она студентка, маши́на, ко́шка, ручка, бразильянка, птица, книга, американка, сумка, дверь, улица
Оно окно, дерево

Chapter 5: Days of the Week, Telling the Time

Кото́рый час?

In this chapter you'll get to know how to talk about time in Russian. We'll also overview days of week and months in Russian. Russian culture obtains a peculiar sence of time. Unlike many European cultures, Russian concept of time is quite relaxed, so be ready that your friend won't turn up exactly on time. It's acceptable if your friend is 15 to 30 minutes late for a party or a casual meeting. For work, business and school the timelines tend to be stricter.

Day – день	Month – месяц	Year – год	Hour - час

Here are some handy expressions to talk about time.

Telling the Time

What time is it?	Кото́рый час?
It's one.	Оди́н час
It's two.	Два часа́
It's three.	Три часа́
It's three ten.	Три часа́ де́сять мину́т
It's four thirty.	Четы́ре три́дцать
It's eight forty-five	Во́семь часо́в со́рок пять мину́т
a.m. (in the morning)	утра́
p.m. (in the afternoon)	дня
p.m. (at night)	вечера́

When you say 1 o'clock and 21 o'clock, you should use the word **час** (1 час, 21 час).

When you say 2 o'clock, 3 o'clock, 4 o'clock, 22 o'clock, 23 o'clock, 24 o'clock you should use the word **часа** (2 часа, 3 часа, 4 часа, 22 часа, 23 часа, 24 часа)

All the rest numbers require the use of the word **часов** (e.g. 5 часов, 8 часов, 11 часов etc.).

Show Your Performance!

What time is it?

1. It's 17:00_____

2. It's 22:00_____
3. It's 5:45_____
4. It's 14:55_____
5 It's 2:15_____
6. It's 11:20_____

Days of the Week

It's good for you to know days of the week in Russian, so you'll be able to help someone who lost track!

What day is it today?	Какой сегодня день?
Today is Monday	Сегодня понедельник
Today	Сегодня
Yesterday	Вчера
Tomorrow	Завтра
Monday	понедельник *m* - понедельник
Tuesday	вторник *m* -
Wednesday	среда *f*
Thursday	четверг *m*
Friday	пятница *f*
Saturday	суббота *f*
Sunday	воскресенье *n*

As you see, one of the features of the Russian language is **Lack of Capitalization.** Many words that are capitalized in English are not capitalized in Russian, for example, days of the week, months, languages and nationalities.

E.g. Tuesday = вторник
February = февраль
Spanish = испанский
Russian = русский

on Monday, on Tuesday etc.: в/во + the accusative case of the Noun denoting a day of the week.

*The accusative case represents the object of an action.

| on Monday | в понедельник *m* |
| on Tuesday | во вторник *m* |

on Wednesday	в среду *f*
on Thursday	в четве́рг *m*
on Friday	в пя́тницу *f*
on Saturday	в суббо́ту *f*
on Sunday	в воскресе́нье *n*

You may have noticed that in the accusative case only feminine days of the week change: they change their ending from -a to -y. Learn it by heart and you'll be able to apply the accusative case to other Nouns on a hunch!

Show Your Performance!

Match English days of the week with their Russian equivalents:

1. on Monday	a. в суббо́ту
2. on Tuesday	b. в четве́рг
3. on Wednesday	c. в понеде́льник
4. on Thursday	d. в воскресе́нье
5. on Friday	e. во вто́рник
6. on Saturday	f. в среду
7. on Sunday	g. в пя́тницу

Talking about the Dates

Have a look at Russian names of months. Pretty similar to English, isn't it? It's as easy as pie!

What is the date today?	Какое сегодня число?
Today is May 15th	Сегодня пятна́дцатое мая
January	янва́рь (января́)
February	февра́ль (февраля́)
March	март (ма́рта)
April	апре́ль (апре́ля)
May	май (ма́я)
June	ию́нь (ию́ня)
July	ию́ль (ию́ля)
August	а́вгуст (а́вгуста)
September	сентя́брь (сентября́)
October	октя́брь (октября́)
November	ноя́брь (ноября́)

| December | дека́брь (декабря́) |

Look at the date in the example above: Today is May 15th. To say it in Russian, you should

- learn the ordinal numbers
-
- learn how to apply the genitive case to the names of the months (in brackets)

Ordinal numbers

1	пе́рвое
2	второ́е
3	тре́тье
4	четвёртое
5	пя́тое
6	шесто́е
7	седьмо́е
8	восьмо́е
9	девя́тое
10	деся́тое
11	оди́ннадцатое
12	двена́дцатое
13	трина́дцатое
14	четы́рнадцатое
15	пятна́дцатое
16	шестна́дцатое
17	семна́дцатое
18	восемна́дцатое
19	девятна́дцатое
20	двадца́тое
21	два́дцать пе́рвое
22, 23, 24, 25, 26, 27, 28, 29	два́дцать …ое
30	тридца́тое
31	три́дцать пе́рвое

Don't worry! They are not as scary as they seem to be! Learning it is no hardship if you sing the ordinal numbers along with the melody of the song *Oh, you dear Augustin*!

All months in Russian are masculine, that's why in the genitive case they have endings

 -а -я , just like neuter ones. For your information, feminine nouns acquire the ending -ы -и .

Show Your Performance!

What day is it today? Translate into English:

Пятое апреля, двадцать шестое января, одиннадцатое мая, двадцать пятое декабря, тридцатое июля, двадцать третье февраля, восьмое марта, девятое сентября, четвертое ноября, тридцать первое октября.

Choose the correct answer:

1. Какое сегодня число?
a. Сегодня понедельник. ---------------------- b. Час дня
c. Пятое апреля -------------------------------- d. В пятницу

2. Сегодня четверг.
a. Today is Monday ---------------------- b. Today is Friday
c. Today is Sunday ---------------------- d. Today is Thursday.

3. Today is April 22
a. Сегодня двадцатое апреля---------------------- b. Сегодня двадцать второе апреля
c. Сегодня двадцатое апрель ---------------------- d. Сегодня двадцать второе апрель

4. It's 10:15.
a. Десять часов шестнадцать минут. ------------------ b. Девять часов пятнадцать минут
c. Девять часов шестнадцать минут. ------------------ d. Десять часов пятнадцать минут

5. It's Sunday, January 14.
a. Суббота, пятнадцатое января ------------------- b. Воскресенье, четырнадцатое января

c. Суббота, четырнадцатое января ---------------d. Воскресенье, пятнадцатое января

Chapter 5: Check Yourself

What time is it?

1. It's 17:00 - Семна́дцать часо́в (пять часо́в ве́чера)
2. It's 22:00 – Два́дцать два часа́ (де́сять часо́в вечера)
3. It's 5:45 – Пять часо́в со́рок пять мину́т
4. It's 14:55 – Четы́рнадцать часо́в пятьдеся́т пять мину́т
5 It's 2:15 – Два ча́са пятна́дцать мину́т
6. It's 11:20 – Оди́ннадцать часо́в два́дцать мину́т

Match English days of the week with their Russian equivalents:

1. on Monday	c. в понеде́льник
2. on Tuesday	e. во вто́рник
3. on Wednesday	f. в сре́ду
4. on Thursday	b. в четве́рг
5. on Friday	g. в пя́тницу
6. on Saturday	a. в суббо́ту
7. on Sunday	d. в воскресенье

What day is it today? Translate into English:

Пятое апреля – April 5, двадцать шестое января - January 26, одиннадцатое мая - May 11, двадцать пятое декабря - December 25, тридцатое июля - July 30, двадцать третье февраля - February 23, восьмое марта - March 8, девятое сентября - September 9, четвертое ноября – November 4, тридцать первое октября - October 31.

Choose the correct answer:

1. Какое сегодня число?
c. Пятое апреля

2. Сегодня четверг.
d. Today is Thursday.

3. Today is April 22
b. Сегодня двадцать второе апреля

4. It's 10:15.
d. Десять часов пятнадцать минут

5. It's Sunday, January 14.
b. Воскресенье, четырнадцатое января

SECTION 2: EVERYDAY LIFE

Chapter 6: Traveling and Transportation

This chapter falls into two sections: *At the Airport* and *Travelling by taxi, bus or train*.

Part 1: At the airport

Imagine how exciting it will be to arrive in a new country, to hear thousands of voices speaking in a foreign language. They will seem to be so relaxed speaking Russian... "What about me?" you may think. - "How am I supposed to understand and speak one of the most difficult languages in the world?". However, there's no reason for you to panic. You are sure to find a person who will be happy to give you a hand! Haven't you heard of Russian hospitality? It may fall beyond your expectations, but Russians are very curious about foreigners: they'll be willing to engage you in conversation and ask you where you are from and what your home is like, and to tell you a bit about theirs. If you practice talking to one person, then – another, you will boost up your language skills, there's no doubt! So, practice, practice and practice! And the airport is the first foreign environment you are going to find yourself in. Although most airport workers are fluent in English, we strongly recommend to start practice your Russian at that point. People will definitely appreciate it!

Therefore, this section discloses the basic words and expressions you need to cope with standard situations at the airport: getting through the customs, dealing with luggage issues, asking about your flight etc. Well, *Приятного полёта!* (Have a good flight!).

Airport Vocabulary

Airport	Рейс
Airplane	Таможня
Airline	Билет
Suitcase	Зона вы́дачи багажа́
Luggage	Вы́ход (на поса́дку)/гейт
Flight	Термина́л
Customs	Па́спорт
Ticket	Пассажи́р
Baggage Claim Area	Рейс
Gate	Таможня
Terminal	Билет

| Passport | Зо́на вы́дачи багажа́ |
| Passenger | Вы́ход (на поса́дку)/гейт |

Useful Phrases at the Airport

When does the flight leave?	Когда́ самолёт вылета́ет?
When does the flight arrive?	Когда́ самолёт прибыва́ет?
I have two suitcases.	У меня́ два чемода́на.
Where is terminal B?	Где термина́л B?
I´m looking for gate 7.	Я ищу́ гейт но́мер семь.
Where is the baggage claim?	Где зо́на вы́дачи багажа́?
My suitcases are lost.	Мой чемода́ны уте́ряны.

Show Your Performance!

Fill in the blanks with the word from the word bank:

Билет   Зона выдачи багажа   Самолет   Чемодан   Авиалиния Паспорт

1. Где _____? Я хочу получить свой багаж.
2. Мой _____ утерян.
3. Мы едем в Москву. Наша _____ - «Аэрофлот».
4. Мой _____ и мой _____ у меня в сумке. Они нужны мне, чтобы сесть на самолет.
5. Когда вылетает мой _____?

Match the English word with the corresponding Russian word:

Airport	Пассажир
Luggage	Терминал
Flight	Аэропорт
Customs	Багаж
Gate	Рейс
Terminal	Выход (на посадку)/гейт
Passenger	Таможня

Translate into English:

A: Добрый вечер! Чем я могу вам помочь?

B: Здравствуйте! Когда вылетает самолет до Екатеринбурга?
A: В 20:55.
B: Спасибо. А какой номер гейта, не подскажете?
A: Номер пятнадцать.
B: Хорошо, большое спасибо!
A: Не за что. Счастливого пути.

Chapter 6: Part 1 Check Yourself

Fill in the blanks using the words from the word bank

1. Где **зона выдачи багажа**? Я хочу получить свой багаж.
2. Мой **чемодан** утерян.
3. Мы едем в Москву. Наша **авиалиния** - «Аэрофлот».
4. Мой **паспорт** и мой **билет** у меня в сумке. Они нужны мне, чтобы сесть на самолет.
5. Когда вылетает мой **самолет**?

Match the English word with the corresponding Russian word:

Airport	j. Аэропорт
Luggage	k. Багаж
Flight	l. Рейс
Customs	n. Таможня
Gate	m. Выход (на посадку)/гейт
Terminal	i. Терминал
Passenger	h. Пассажир

Translation

A: Good evening! How can I help you?
B: Hello! When does the flight to Yekaterinburg leave?
A: At 20:55.
B: Thanks. And could you tell the gate number?
A: It's #15.
B: Good, thank you very much!
A: You're welcome. Have a good trip!

Part 2: Traveling by taxi, bus, or train.

Once you step out of the airport, the chances to meet an English-speaking person diminish. As the saying goes, в *Тулу со своим самоваром не ездят* (Nobody goes to Tula with one's own samovar). By the way, Tula is a city famous for the best Russian samovars. So you'll have to adjust and start speaking Russian right away! The aim of this section is to teach you some basic words and phrases related to transport that runs in and outside the Russian cities. Remember how to call populated localities in Russian:

город (city, town)
село (a village with a church)
деревня (a village with no church; countryside)

In addition there's a word **дача** (dacha) that describes a piece of land in the outskirts where Russians have a country house, grow fruit, vegetables and flowers and relax their mind, body and soul.

In this section we'll also touch upon one of the most difficult grammar aspects of the Russian language – the <u>verb conjugation.</u>

As you might have noticed, Russian verbs change depending on their subject not only in the 1st person singular of the present tense as in English (e..g. he go**es**, she like**s** etc.). Each person and number of the subject requires special verb endings. This is called <u>verb conjugation.</u>

The basic form of the verb, or the infinitive, in Russian generally ends with **–ть**, and sometimes with **–ти, -чь, -ться, -чься**. The equivalent of these Russian endings is the English particle **to,** e.g. **to do** (дела**ть**).

Now we are going to conjugate the following verbs: **идти** - to go on foot and **ехать** - to go by transport.

	идти (to go on foot)	éхать (to go by bike, car, bus etc.)	кудá?(where to?)
I go	я идý	я еду	в университéт (to University)
You go	ты идёшь	ты éдешь	в музей (to the museum)
He/She/It goes	Он/онá идёт	Он/онá éдет	на пóчту (to the post

54

			office)
We go	мы идём	мы éдем	на рынок (to the market)
You guys go (or formal)	вы идёте	вы éдете	в аптéку (to the drugstore)
They go	они́ иду́т	они́ éдут	на дискотéку (to the disco)
...m went, ... f went, (we, you (pl.), they) went	я, ты, он шёл; m я, ты, она шла, f мы, вы, они шли(pl.)	я, ты, он éхал; m я, ты, она́ éхала, f мы, вы, они́ éхали (pl.)	домóй (home)

The Nouns from the column **куда?(where to?)** are given in the indicative case. As it was mentioned in the chapter on Telling Time, only feminine Nouns change their endings: from -**a** into -**y**. Find these Nouns and put them into the Nominative (basic) case.

Here is the answer: почт**а**, аптек**а**, дискотек**а**.

Consider that you don't have to use the personal pronouns (я, ты, он, она etc.) all the time. It's clear who you are talking about because information about the person is implied in the form of the verb, especially in its ending:

E. g. I go = ид**у** (No need to always say *я иду*)

You go = ид**ёшь** (No need to always say *ты идешь*)

Taxi Vocabulary

Taxi will probably be your main means of traveling around the city. Its pros are the opportunity to practice your language skills and the chance to learn more about the surroundings from your "personal guide". Taxi drivers in Russia are typically as garrulous as magpies (трещат, как сороки)! So all you have to do is to ask questions showing your interest and prick up your ears!

Where are we going?	Куда́ мы éдем?
I'm going to...	Я еду в (на) ...

Turn right/left at the traffic lights	Поверните направо/налево после светофора
You can stop here.	Можете остановиться здесь.
It's here, on the right/left	Это здесь, справа/слева.
How much do I owe you?	Сколько я вам должен?

Show Your Performance!

Put the verb *идти* in the correct form.

1. Я завтра _____ на дискотеку.

2. Куда мы _____?

3. Ты сегодня _____ в музей?

4. Куда она _____?

5. Вы _____ домой? (formal)

Say it in Russian using the verb *идти*:

E.g. Маша - - - - - - - - - - - > магазин
Маша идёт в магазин
Александр - - - - - - - - - - - > дом
Мы - - - - - - - - - - - > университет
Они - - - - - - - - - - - > дискотека
Я - - - - - - - - - - - > аптека
Настя и Антон - - - - - - - - - - - > рынок

Put the verb *ехать* in the correct form.

1. Я сегодня _____ на почту.
2. Куда они _____?
3. Вы завтра _____ в университет? (formal)
4. Куда он _____?
5. Мы _____ на рынок?

Say it in Russian using the verb *ехать*:

E.g. Маша - - - - - - - - - - - > магазин
Маша едет в магазин
Александр - - - - - - - - - - - > дом
Мы - - - - - - - - - - - > университет
Они - - - - - - - - - - - > дискотека
Я - - - - - - - - - - - > аптека
Настя и Антон - - - - - - - - - - - > рынок

Match the phrase in English with the corresponding phrase in Russian:

1. Where are we going?	a) Можете остановиться здесь.
2. I'm going to...	b) Поверните направо/налево после светофора
3. Turn right/left at the traffic lights	c) Я еду в (на) ...
4. You can stop here.	d) Сколько я вам должен?
5. It's here, on the right/left	e) Куда едем?
6. How much do I owe you?	f) Это здесь, справа/слева.

Bus and Train Vocabulary

You will most likely travel by train to get from a city to a village or to another city. But there also are land cruisers and shuttle buses traveling between cities.

Bus station	Автовокза́л
Train station	Железнодоро́жный вокза́л (ж/д вокза́л)
Bus stop	(Авто́бусная) остано́вка
When does the next train leave for...?	Во ско́лько (уезжа́ет) сле́дующий по́езд в ...?
Arrivals	Прибы́тие
Departures	Отправле́ние
A one way ticket, please	Биле́т в оди́н коне́ц, пожа́луйста
A round trip ticket, please	Биле́т в о́ба конца́, пожа́луйста
Which platform does the train leave from?	С како́й платфо́рмы уезжа́ет по́езд?
Do I need to change trains?	Мне ну́жно сде́лать переса́дку?
To get on...	Сади́ться на ...
To get off...	Выходи́ть из ...
Have a good trip!	Счастли́вого пути́!

Verb Conjugation

Here's the conjugation of the verb **уезжать** (to leave).

In Russian, you can leave some place (уезжать из, с, от) and can also leave **for** (уезжать в, на) some place.

In the first case, you should mix the second column with the third one - **откуда? (where from?)** column below.

E.g. Я уезжаю из Москвы (из дома, от Марии). = I'm leaving Moscow (home, Maria's place).

In the second case, you may still use the fourth column **куда? (where to?)** from the conjugation table of the verbs *идти* and *ехать*.

E.g. Я уезжаю в Германию (в аптеку, на рынок). = I'm leaving for Germany (the drugstore, the market).

	уезжа́ть (to leave)	отку́да? (where from?)
I leave	я уезжа́ю	из Москвы́
You leave	ты уезжа́ешь	из до́ма
He/She/It leaves	Он/она́ уезжа́ет	от Ма́кса
We leave	мы уезжа́ем	из Шереметьево
You guys leave (or formal)	вы уезжа́ете	от Мари́и
They leave	они́ уезжа́ют	из Петербу́рга
(He) left, (she) left, (we, they) left	уе́хал, уе́хала, уе́хали	от роди́телей

Pay attention to the use of the prepositions: we take **из/с** if there follows a name of a country, city or a place, and **от** if we mention a person or people, whose place we visited (от друзей, от родителей, от Макса).

The column where from? is given in the genitive case that we mentioned before. Feminine Nouns change the ending -а, -я into -ы, -и; neuter and masculine Nouns generally change the ending into -а. Plural forms often end with -ей, -ов.

E. g. Мы уезжаем **из** Турции. = We are leaving Turkey.

Мы уехали **от** друзей. = We left our friends' place.

Show Your Performance!

Put the verb *уезжать* in the correct form.

1. Я _____ в Германию.
2. Во сколько _____ следующий поезд в Новгород?
3. Ты скоро _____ от Наташи?
4. Он _____ из Шереметьево в 3 часа.
5. Во сколько они _____ в деревню?

Say it in Russian using the verb *уезжать* paying attention to the direction *куда* or *откуда*:

E.g. Маша - - - - - - - - - - - -> магазин
Маша уезжает в магазин
Маша <- - - - - - - - - - - - магазин
Маша уезжает из магазина

Александр - - - - - - - - - - - -> дом
Мы <- - - - - - - - - - - - университет
Они - - - - - - - - - - - -> дискотека
Я - - - - - - - - - - - -> Ту́ла
Настя и Антон - - - - - - - - - - - -> рынок
Мы с Анной <- - - - - - - - - - - - Макс

Translate into English:

A: Добрый день! Чем я могу вам помочь?
B: Когда будет ближайший поезд в Петербург?
A: Сегодня в 6 вечера.
B: Спасибо. Я хотел бы билет до Петербурга в один конец, пожалуйста.
A: Хорошо.
B: С какой платформы уезжает поезд?
A: С третьей.
B: Отлично, большое спасибо.
A: Не за что. Счастливого пути.

Chapter 6: Part 2 Check Yourself

Put the verb *идти* in the correct form.

1. Я завтра **иду** на дискотеку.
2. Куда мы **идём**?
3. Ты сегодня **идёшь** в музей?
4. Куда она **идёт**?
5. Вы **идёте** домой? (formal)

Say it in Russian using the verb *идти*:

E.g. Маша - - - - - - - - - - - > магазин
Маша идёт в магазин
Александр **идёт** дом**ой**
Мы **идём в** университет
Они **идут на** дискотек**у**
Я **иду в** аптек**у**
Настя и Антон **идут на** рынок

Put the verb *ехать* in the correct form.

1. Я сегодня **еду** на почту.
2. Куда они **едут**?
3. Вы завтра **едете** в университет? (formal)
4. Куда он **едет**?
5. Мы **едем** на рынок?

Say it in Russian using the verb *ехать*:

Александр **едет** дом**ой**.
Мы **едем в** университет.
Они **едут на** дискотек**у**.
Я **еду в** аптек**у**.
Настя и Антон **едут на** рынок.

Match the phrase in English with the corresponding phrase in Russian:

1. Where are we going?	e) Куда едем?
2. I'm going to...	c) Я еду в (на) ...
3. Turn right/left at the traffic lights	b) Поверните направо/налево после светофора

4. You can stop here.	a) Можете остановиться здесь.
5. It's here, on the right/left	f) Это здесь, справа/слева.
6. How much do I owe you?	d) Сколько я вам должен?

Put the verb *уезжать* in the correct form

1. Я завтра **уезжаю** в Германию.
2. Во сколько **уезжает** следующий поезд в Новгород?
3. Ты скоро **уезжаешь** от Наташи?
4. Он **уезжает** из Шереметьево в 3 часа.
5. Во сколько они **уезжают** в деревню?

Say it in Russian using the verb *уезжать* paying attention to the direction куда or откуда:

Александр **уезжает** дом**ой**. = Alexander is going home.
Мы **уезжаем из** университет**а**. = We are leaving the Univesrity.
Они **уезжают на** дискотек**у**. = They are going to the disco.
Я **уезжаю в** Тул**у**. = I'm going to Tula.
Настя и Антон **уезжают на** рынок. = Nastya and Anton are going to the market.
Мы с Анной **уезжаем от** Макс**а**. = Anna and I are leaving Max.

Translation

A: Good afternoon, how can I help you?
B: What time does the next train leave for St. Petersburg?
A: Today at 6:30 in the evening.
B: Thank you. I would like a round trip ticket to St. Petersburg, please.
A: All right.
B: Which platform does the train leave from?
A: From platform 3.
B: Great, thank you very much.
A: You're welcome, have a good trip.

Chapter 7: Asking For Directions (Excuse Me, Where Is the...?)

Где здесь библиотека?

So, you got off the taxi or the bus, and you find yourself in new surroundings! You need some expressions to get your bearings and find your destination. Or you are simply looking for a new attraction in the city and need to ask a passer-by. At this time, everyone has smartphones with maps and GPS, but you'll anyway need to stop and ask for directions from time to time. Moreover, Wifi is not so widely distributed in Russian-speaking countries, and you will not have such straightforward access to the Internet when you are in the city or in the countryside.

Directions

Memorize the most useful words and phrases for asking where some places in town are.

Where is ... over here?	Где здесь ...?
Excuse me, where is the...	Простите, где ...?
It's next to the...	Рядом с ...
It's in front of the...	Перед ...
Go straight on	Идите прямо
Turn right at...	Поверните направо
Turn left at....	Поверните налево
On the right/left	Справа / слева
Far from	Далеко от...
Near to	Близко к...
Above	Над
Below	Под
Behind	За

Places

The good thing about asking where some places are is that you have only to say

Где + name of the place There are no verbs and articles, remember?

The hotel	отéль *m* (отéл**ем**)
The hostel	хóстел *m* (хóстел**ом**)

The restaurant	ресторáн *m* (ресторáн**ом**)
The post office	пóчта *f* (пóчт**ой**)
The library	библиотéка *f* (библиотéк**ой**)
The supermarket	супермáркет *m* (супермáркет**ом**)
The pharmacy	аптéка *f* (аптéк**ой**)
The bakery	пекáрня *f* (пекáрн**ей**)
Bus stop	автóбусная остановка *f* (автóбусн**ой** остановк**ой**)
Store	магазúн *m* (магазúн**ом**)
Church	цéрковь *f* (цéрковь**ю**)
Embassy	посóльство *n* (посóльств**ом**)

When you want to say e.g. *in front of the hotel* or *near to the church*, you should apply the <u>instrumental</u> case (in brackets) to the Nouns *hotel* and *church*. This case is aimed to denote an instrument that helps to do something.

The masculine and neutral Nouns get the ending ─ом ─ем , the feminine Nouns get the ending ─ой ─ей ─ю .

E.g. in front of the hotel = перед отел**ем**; near to the church = рядом с церковь**ю**; behind the supermarket = за супермаркет**ом**.

Other Phrases

I am lost.	Я заблудúлся / заблудúлась
How do I get to …?	Как мне добрáться до …?
Cross the street.	Перейдúте ýлицу.
Where am I now?	Где я сейчáс?
the corner	ýгол
round the corner	за углóм
street	ýлица
outside	на ýлице
here	здесь
there	там

Time Expressions

Before	до
Now	сейчáс

After	по́сле
Later/Then	пото́м

*You may use *(вы) не подскажете?* (won't you tell...?) in any question that you ask in the street, in the supermarket, at the airport etc. The good thing about it is that you only have to name the subject you are interested in, adding *не подскажете?* either at the beginning or at the end of the sentence.

E.g. **Не подскажете**, который час? = Который час, **не подскажете**? (Can you tell what time it is?)

Вы не подскажете номер телефона Анатолия? = Номер телефона Анатолия **не подскажете**? (Can you tell Anatoly's phone number?)

Show Your Performance!

Choose the correct answer

1. The restaurant is next to the post office.
a. Ресторан рядом с почта.-------------- b. Ресторан рядом с почтой.
c. Ресторан рядом с посольство.----- d. Ресторан рядом с посольством.

2. Turn left, the bus stop is round the corner.
a. Поверните направо, автобусная остановка за углом.
b. Поверните направо, автобусная остановка возле магазина.
c. Поверните налево, автобусная остановка за углом.
d. Поверните налево, автобусная остановка возле магазина.

3. The bakery is close to the hotel.
a. Пекарня рядом с отелем.-------- b. Отель рядом с пекарня.
c. Отель далеко от пекарня.---------d. Пекарня рядом с отель.

Read aloud, guess the meaning of the new words and translate into English:

#1

A: Извини́те, где хостел?
B: Поверни́те напра́во, зате́м нале́во у це́ркви.
A: OK.
B: Хо́стел за суперма́ркетом.
A: Спаси́бо!

#2
A: Извини́те, я заблуди́лся. Как мне добра́ться до посо́льства?
B: Иди́те пря́мо, зате́м поверни́те напра́во у магази́на.
A: Хорошо́.
B: Посо́льство ря́дом с магази́ном.
A: Спаси́бо!
B: Не́ за что!

Chapter 7: Check Yourself

Choose the correct answer:

1. The restaurant is next to the post office.
b. Ресторан рядом с почтой.

2. Turn left, the bus stop is round the corner.
c. Поверните налево, автобусная остановка за углом.

3. The bakery is close to the hotel.
a. Пекарня рядом с отелем.

Read aloud, guess the meaning of the new words and translate into English:
#1
A: Excuse me, where is the hostel?
B: Turm right, and then turn left at the church.
A: OK.
B: The hostel is behind the supermarket.
A: Thanks!
#2
A: Excuse me, I'm lost. How do I get to the embassy?
B: Go straight on, and then turn right at the store.
A: All right.
B: The embassy is next to the store.
A: Thanks!
B: You are welcome!

Chapter 8: Eating Out (Food + Restaurants)

Я хотел бы...

You are surely starving by this moment! So, it's chow time at last! You'll need some basic expressions to easily cope with menus in cafes and restaurants, to be able to choose, order, express preferences and ask questions about meals. They say, *Аппетит приходит во время еды* (The appetite comes with eating), and so it is! The more Russian food you try, the more you want! You are about to learn how to ask for second helping if you don't feel stuffed after having a nourishing холодец (kholodets), щи (shchi) and окрошка (okroshka). If you really like the meal you should say *вкусно!* (tasty!)

You may specify if you want your water sparkling (с газом) or still (без газа) what means water with or without gas. As all the Russians say before starting the meal: «Приятного аппетита!» (Bon appétit!).

There are three major meals during the day:

Breakfast	Завтрак *m*
Lunch	Обед *m*
Dinner	Ужин *m*

Verb Conjugation

Here is the conjugation of the most important verb in all languages – любить (to love). It will help you to show your preferences in food and beverages. In Russian people usually use the verb *love* instead of *like* when talking about food.

	любить (to love)	что? (what?)
I love	я люблю	яблоки *n pl* (apples)
You love	ты любишь	бананы *m pl* (bananas)
He/She/It loves	Он/она любит	курицу *f* (chicken)
We love	мы любим	суп *m* (soup)
You guys love (or formal)	вы любите	бифштекс *m* (beefsteak)
They love	они любят	сыр *m* (cheese)
(He) loved, (she) loved, (we, they) loved	любил, любила, любили	мороженое *n* (ice-

		cream) пиццу *f* (pizza) красное вино *n* (red wine)

What's the case of the Nouns in the third column? Right, accusative! You should have determined by the fact that only feminine nouns changed, and they have the ending -у

To say that you <u>don't</u> like something you should put the particle НЕ before the verb:

E.g. I love apples = я люблю яблоки

I don't like apples = я **не** люблю яблоки

Show Your Performance!

Say it in Russian:

1. I love red wine.
2. They love apples.
3. Do you like (=love) pizza?
4. He likes chicken.
5. We love soup and salad.
6. I don't like pasta.
7. He doesn't like ice-cream.
8. They don't like soup.

Restaurant phrases

The well-known saying *Аппетит приходит во время еды* can be taken both directly and figuratively. The more you learn Russian, the more you want to keep on! Here are some phrases that will prevent you from leaving the restaurant with an empty stomach!

What can I bring to you?	Что вам принести?
I would like to eat…	Я хотéл бы съесть … + Noun in the genitive case
I would like to drink…	Я хотéл бы вы́пить … + Noun in the genitive case

Menu, please	Меню, пожа́луйста.
What do you recommend?	Что́ вы порекоменду́ете?
Can you bring …?	Вы мо́жете принести́…?
Excuse me, sir!	Извини́те, молодо́й челове́к!
Excuse me, ma'am!	Извини́те, де́вушка!
Drink	Напи́ток
A glass	Стака́н
Soft Drinks	Безалкого́льные напи́тки
Juice	Сок
A glass of water	Стака́н воды́
Beer	Пи́во
A glass of wine	Бока́л вина́
Dessert	Десе́рт
Tips	Чаевы́е
The check, please	Счёт, пожа́луйста
So/then	Так / ита́к

Food Vocabulary

What are the ingredients in the dish?	Каки́е здесь ингредие́нты?
Is there … in the dish?	Здесь есть …?
Meat	Мя́со *n*
Fish	Ры́ба *f*
Chicken	Ку́рица *f*
Ham	Ветчина́ *f*
Egg (eggs)	Яйцо́ (я́йца) *n*
Pasta	Па́ста (лапша́) *f (f)*
Salad	Сала́т *m*
Bread	Хлеб *m*
Cheese	Сыр *m*
Vegetables	О́вощи *m pl*
Fruit	Фру́кты *m pl*
Rice	Рис *m*
Milk	Молоко́ *n*
A lot, much, many	Мно́го
Few, little	Ма́ло

The Russian verb *есть* is an equivalent of the Englsih construction there is / there are; it is possible to leave it out however.

The verb есть = There is/There are E.g. (Есть) много хлеба и сыра = There is a lot of bread and cheese.

На обед (есть) лапша и курица = For lunch, there is pasta and chicken.

The construction *У меня есть*

This verb can also be used in the meaning *to have*. Have a look at the table:

		что? (what?) кто? (who?)
I have	у меня есть	муж *m* (a husband)
You have	у тебя есть	жена *f* (a wife)
He/She/It has	у него есть/у неё есть	питомец *m* (a pet)
We have	у нас есть	дом *m* (a house)
You guys have (or formal)	у вас есть	время *n* (time)
They have	у них есть	деньги *always pl* (money)
(He) had, (she) had, (we, they) had	у него был, у неё был, у них был	любимое блюдо *n* (favorite dish)

E.g. I have a wife. = У меня есть женá.
They have a house. = У них есть дом.
She has a pet. = У неё есть питомец.

This construction is convenient for you for the reason that the Noun after *есть* is always in the Nominative (basic) case. Tell your friends what you have in Russian! In the next chapter you'll learn how to say that you don't have something.

Show Your Performance!

Match the phrases in English with their Russian equivalents:

1. Can you bring …?	a. Что вы порекомендуете?
2. Is there … in the dish?	b. Вы можете принести…?
3. What do you recommend?	c. Какие здесь ингредиенты?
4. What are the ingredients in the dish?	d. Что вам принести?
5. What can I bring to you?	e. Здесь есть …?

Choose the correct answer:

1. There are fish, vegetables, and pasta in the dish.
a. В блюде рыба, овощи и рис.
b. В блюде мало рыбы, пасты и овощей.
c. В блюде рыба, паста и фрукты.
d. В блюде рыба, овощи и паста.

2. В блюде есть много мяса.
a. There is little meat in the dish.
b. There is a lot if meat in the dish.
c. There isn't a lot if meat in the dish.
d. There is no meat in the dish.

3. Excuse me ma'am, the check please.
a. Извините, девушка, бокал вина, пожалуйста.
b. Извините, молодой человек, стакан молока, пожалуйста.
c. Извините, девушка, счёт, пожалуйста.
d. Извините, молодой человек, счёт, пожалуйста.

4. На завтрак – фруктовый салат и йогурт.
a. There is vegetable salad and yogurt for breakfast.
b. There is fruit salad and yogurt for breakfast.
c. There is salad and corn flakes for breakfast.
d. There is fruit salad and a croissant for breakfast.

5. После обеда я хотел бы десерт.
a. I would like a dessert before lunch.
b. I would like a dessert after lunch.
c. I would like some wine after lunch.
d. I would like a dessert 2 hours after lunch.

Read aloud and translate into Englsih:

У неё есть муж. У него́ есть жена́. У них есть де́ньги. У нас есть пито́мец. У меня́ есть вре́мя. У вас есть сала́т? У вас есть люби́мое блю́до? Что э́то?

Read aloud, guess the meaning of new words, and translate into Englsih:

A: До́брый ве́чер. Что вам принести́?

B: До́брый ве́чер, а что́ вы порекомендуете?
A: Вы лю́бите ку́рицу?
B: Да, люблю́.
A: Тогда́ рекоменду́ю э́тот сала́т с ку́рицей и анана́сом.
B: Это вку́сно?
A: Да, э́то о́чень вку́сно.
B: Хорошо́, тогда́ я хоте́л бы э́то блю́до.
A: Что́ вы бу́дете пить?
B: Стака́н воды без га́за.
A: Хорошо́.
B: Спаси́бо.

Chapter 8: Check Yourself

Say it in Russian:

1. I love red wine. = Я люблю красное вино.
2. They love apples. = Они любят яблоки.
3. Do you like (=love) pizza? = Ты любишь пиццу?
4. He likes chicken. = Он любит курицу?
5. We love soup and salad. = Мы любим суп и салат.
6. I don't like pasta. Я не люблю пасту.
7. He doesn't like ice-cream. Он не любит мороженое.
8. They don't like soup. Они не любят суп.

Choose the correct answer

1. There is fish, vegetables, and pasta in the dish.
d. В блюде рыба, овощи и паста.

2. В блюде есть много мяса.
b. There is a lot if meat in the dish.

3. Excuse me ma'am, the check please.
c. Извините, девушка, счёт, пожалуйста.

4. На завтрак — фруктовый салат и йогурт.
b. There is fruit salad and yogurt for breakfast.

5. После обеда я хотел бы десерт.
b. I would like a dessert after lunch.

Read aloud and translate into Englsih:

У неё есть муж. У него есть жена. У них есть деньги. У нас есть питомец. У меня есть время. У вас есть салат? У вас есть любимое блюдо? Что это?

She has got a husband. He has got a wife. They have got money. We have got a pet. I have got time. Have you got a salad? Have you got a favorite dish? What is it?

Match the phrases in English with their Russian equivalents:

1.	Can you bring …?	b. Вы можете принести…?
2.	Is there … in the dish?	e. Здесь есть …?
3.	What do you recommend?	a. Что вы порекомендуете?
4.	What are the ingredients in the dish?	c. Какие здесь ингредиенты?
5.	What can I bring to you?	d. Что вам принести?

Read aloud, guess the meaning of new words, and translate into Englsih:

A: Good evening. What can I bring to you?
B: Good evening, and what do you recommend?
A: Do you like chicken?
B: Yes, I love it.
A: Then I recommend this salad with chicken and pineapple.
B: Is it tasty?
A: Yes, it's very tasty.
B: Well, then I would like this dish.
A: What would you like to drink?
B: A glass of water without gas.
A: Okay.
B: Thank you.

Chapter 9: Let's Go Shopping!

Сколько это стоит?

So, you found your legs in a new country, you saw lots of attractions, you enjoyed great local food, and you are charmed by local people... What's next? You probably wish to go shopping because you need to take something tangible back home to your friends, family, colleagues, or just for yourself. You may also need to buy clothes for the Russian weather, e.g. a winter coat or a Russian hat, because winters there are absolutely freezing, especially in Siberia.

The most common units of trade are stores, supermarkets and malls, so you can always find the price of the thing you want on the label. But there still are some markets and trade fairs of hand-made stuff, for example, where you certainly need to be able to ask basic questions and even bargain with the seller, why not? Here are the basic phrases that can help you to find what you are looking for and to get good deals with pleasure.

Shopping phrases

How can I help you?	Чем (я) могу́ (вам) помо́чь?
How much does it cost?	Ско́лько э́то сто́ит?
How much is it?	Ско́лько сто́ит ...?
Which one do you want?	Како́й *m* /каку́ю *f* вы хоти́те?
I would like that one.	Я хоте́л(а) бы тот *m*/ ту *f*.
It's too expensive.	Э́то сли́шком до́рого.
It's cheap.	Э́то дёшево.
Do you have...?	У вас есть ...?
Do you have bigger/smaller?	У вас есть ... побо́льше/поме́ньше?
Do you accept credit cards?	Вы принима́ете креди́тные ка́рты?
We only accept cash.	Мы принима́ем то́лько нали́чные.
(Where) can I try it on?	(Где) мо́жно приме́рить?
I'm just looking.	Я про́сто смотрю́.
Sale	Распрода́жа
Discount	Ски́дка
Discount card	Диско́нтная ка́рта
Of course!	Коне́чно!

The construction *У меня нет*

As it was promised in the previous chapter, we are going to learn how to say *I don't have...* The things here are a bit more complicated, because the noun after **нет** is used in the genitive case.

		чего? (what?) кого? (who?) **Genitive case:**
I haven't got	у меня нет	мужа *m* (a husband)
You haven't got	у тебя нет	жены *f* (a wife)
He/She/It has	у него нет /у неё нет	питомца *m* (a pet)
We haven't got	у нас нет	дома *m* (a house)
You guys haven't got (or formal)	у вас нет	времени *n* (time)
They haven't got	у них нет	денег *always pl* (money)
(He) hadn't got, (she) hadn't got, (we, they) hadn't got	у него не́ было, у неё не́ было, у них не́ было	любимого блюда *n* (favorite dish)

E.g. I haven't got a wife. = У меня нет жен**ы́**.
They haven't got a house. = У них нет д**о́**м**а**.
She hasn't got a pet. = У неё нет питомц**а**.

Shopping Vocabulary

These are the most common objects of shopping you may be looking for:

souvenir	сувени́р *m*
keychain	брело́к *m*
shirt	руба́шка *f*
T-shirt	футбо́лка *f*
pants	брю́ки *always pl*
shorts	шо́рты *always pl*
a dress	пла́тье *n*
a jacket	ку́ртка *f*
shoes	ту́фли *pl*
a cap	ке́пка *f*
a hat	ша́пка *f*
a fur coat	шу́ба *f*
a Russian hat	уша́нка *f*
boots	сапоги́ *pl*
sweater	сви́тер *m*

Note that the words *pants, shorts, jeans* etc. are also plural in Russian. So you can interchange them with the pronoun **они**. It is typical for Russian plural Nouns to have endings -и -ы E.g. брюк**и**, сапог**и**, штан**ы**, сувенир**ы**

Sometimes when you don't know how to call a thing, you may say штука *f* (thing). Below there's a list of the demonstrative adjectives in Russian (this, that, these, those) since we use them quite often when doing shopping, 'I would like this/that thing, please'.

Demonstrative Adjectives (This, That, These, Those)

Demonstrative Adjectives in Russian change their form according to the gender, the case and the number of the following noun.

This and That

If you want to say, for example, *this boy*, use one of the three forms of the Russian word *that* according to the gender of the noun. The accusative case is in brackets. As it usually happens with the accusative case, only feminine Nouns change their form.

English	Masculine	Feminine	Neutral (When you don't know}
This	Этот (э́тот)	Эта (э́ту)	Это (э́то)
That	Тот (тот)	Та (ту)	То (то)

E.g. этот мальчик = this boy *m*
эта улица = this street *f*
тот дом = that house *m*
та женщина = that woman *f*
это окно = this window *n*
то место = that place *n*

I would like this thing = я хотел *m*/хотела *f* бы эту штуку
I would like that thing = я хотел *m* / хотела *f* бы ту штуку
Give me this/ that thing, please = дайте мне эту / ту штуку, пожалуйста

These and Those

In plural forms we don't take into account the gender of the noun. These pronouns also do not change their form in the accusative case.

English	Masculine	Feminine	Gender Neutral
These	Эти	Эти	Эти
Those	Те	Те	Те

E.g. эти мальчики = these boys
эти улицы = these streets
те дома = those houses
те женщины = those women etc.

I would like these things = я хотел *m*/хотела *f* бы эти штуки
I would like those things = я хотел *m* / хотела *f* бы те штуки
Give me these/ those things, please = дайте мне эти / те штуки, пожалуйста

Show Your Performance!

Read aloud and translate into Englsih:

У неё нет мужа. У него нет жены. У них нет денег. У нас нет питомца. У меня нет времени. У вас нет любимого блюда? У вас нет шубы? У него нет шортов. У меня нет ушанки. У неё нет платья.

Say it in Russian using the right form of the demonstrative pronoun:

This dress, these shoes, that shirt, this jacket, that cap, those T-shirts, these souvenirs, those boots, that sweater, this fur coat, this keychain.

Choose the correct answer

1. Шапки
a. эта.-------b. это
c. этот .-----d. эти

2. I would like these shoes.
a. Я хотела бы тот туфли.----- b. Я хотела бы ту туфли.

c. Я хотела бы те туфли.------- d. Я не хотела бы те туфли.

3. Do you have bigger fur coats?
a. У вас есть шубы побольше?----- b. У вас есть ушанки побольше?
c. У вас есть шубы поменьше?----- d. У вас есть ушанки поменьше?

Read aloud, guess the meaning of the new words and translate into English:

A: Здра́вствуйте, чем могу́ помо́чь?
B: Я просто смотрю́, спаси́бо.
A: Не́ за что.
B: Ско́лько сто́ит э́та руба́шка?
A: Семь ты́сяч пятьсо́т рубле́й.
B: Это о́чень до́рого! А э́ти джи́нсы?
A: Две ты́сячи рубле́й.
B: Я могу́ их приме́рить?
A: Коне́чно!
A: Вы принима́ете креди́тки?
B: Нет, принима́ем то́лько нали́чные.
A: Две ты́сячи рубле́й.
B: Хорошо́, большо́е спаси́бо.

Chapter 9: Check Yourself

Read aloud and translate into Englsih:

У неё нет му́жа. У него́ нет жены́. У них нет де́нег. У нас нет пито́мца. У меня́ нет вре́мени. У вас нет люби́мого блю́да? У вас нет шу́бы? У него́ нет шо́ртов. У меня́ нет уша́нки. У неё нет пла́тья.

She hasn't got a husband. He hasn't got a wife. They haven't got money. We haven't got a pet. I haven't got time. Haven't you got a favorite dish? Haven't you got a fur coat? He hasn't got any shorts. I haven't got an ushanka. She hasn't got a dress.

Say it in Russian using the right form of the demonstrative pronoun:

This dress, these shoes, that shirt, this jacket, that cap, those T-shirts, these souvenirs, those boots, that sweater, this fur coat, this keychain.

Это платье, эти туфли, эта рубашка, эта куртка, та кепка, те футболки, эти сувениры, те сапоги, тот свитер, эта шуба, этот брелок.

Choose the correct answer

1. Шапки
d. эти

2. I would like these shoes.
c. Я хотела бы эти туфли.

3. Do you have bigger fur coats?
a. У вас есть шубы побольше?

Read aloud, guess the meaning of the new words and translate into English:

A: Good morning, how can I help you?
B: I'm just looking, thanks.
A: You are welcome.
B: How much does this shirt cost?
A: 7500 rubles.
B: It's very expensive! What about these jeans?
A: 2000 rubles.
B: Can I try them on?
A: Sure!
B: Do you accept credit cards?
A: No, we only accept cash.
B: OK, thank you very much.

Chapter 10: Finding a Place to Stay

Где остановиться на ночь?

You should have arrived at your destination by now, whatever it took you! Hope you didn't get into trouble or get lost. It doesn't matter anyway, because it's probably getting dark (especially if it's winter, and the day is very short), and you suddenly realize that you have no place to stay! Look around for some signs like ОТЕЛЬ (Hotel), ГОСТИНИЦА (Inn), ХОСТЕЛ (Hostel), СДАЮ (for rent) and get ready to ask questions. No fuss! We've got some handy phrases for ya! Enjoy your stay!

Hotel Vocabulary

I would like to reserve a room for one/two people.	Я хотéл(а) бы забронировать нóмер на одногó / двух человéк.
How much does it cost per night?	Какáя цена́ зá ночь?
For how many people?	На скóлько человéк?
For how many nights?	На скóлько ночéй?
For one night/two nights	На одну́ ночь / две ночи .
With a double bed.	С двуспáльной кровáтью.
With twin beds.	С двумя́ односпáльными кровáтями.
I'm sorry, we are full.	Мне óчень жаль, мест нет.
I have a reservation.	Я брониров́ал нóмер.
Do you have Wi-Fi?	У вас есть Wi-Fi?

Show Your Performance!

Match the phrase in English with the corresponding phrase in Russian:

1. I would like to reserve a room for one/two people.	a. С двуспáльной кровáтью.
2. How much does it cost per night?	b. С двумя́ односпáльными кровáтями.
3. For how many people?	c. Мне óчень жаль, мест нет.
4. For how many nights?	d. Я бронировал нóмер.
5. For one night/two nights	e. У вас есть Wi-Fi?
6. With a double bed.	f. Я хотéл(а) бы забронировать нóмер на одногó / двух человéк.
7. With twin beds.	g. Какáя цена́ зá ночь?

8. I'm sorry, we are full.	h. На сколько человек?
9. I have a reservation.	i. На сколько ночей?
10. Do you have Wi-Fi?	j. На одну ночь / две ночи.

Read aloud, guess the meaning of new words and translate into English:

A: Добрый вечер!
B: Добрый вечер! Чем я могу вам помочь?
A: Я хотел бы забронировать номер на двоих человек.
B: На сколько ночей?
A: На пять.
B: Хорошо.
A: А какая цена за ночь?
B: 2100 рублей.
A: А у вас есть Wi-Fi?
B: Нет, у нас нет Wi-Fi.
A: Ладно, спасибо.

Chapter 10: Check Yourself

Match the phrase in English with the corresponding phrase in Russian:

1. I would like to reserve a room for one/two people.	f. Я хотел(а) бы забронировать номер на одного / двух человек.
2. How much does it cost per night?	g. Какая цена за ночь?
3. For how many people?	h. На сколько человек?
4. For how many nights?	i. На сколько ночей?
5. For one night/two nights	j. На одну ночь / две ночи.
6. With a double bed.	a. С двуспальной кроватью.
7. With twin beds.	b. С двумя односпальными кроватями.
8. I'm sorry, we are full.	c. Мне очень жаль, мест нет.
9. I have a reservation.	d. Я бронировал номер.
10. Do you have Wi-Fi?	e. У вас есть Wi-Fi?

Read aloud, guess the meaning of new words and translate into English:

A: Good evening!
B: Good evening! How can I help you??
A: I would like to reserve a room for two people.

B: For how many nights?
A: For five nights.
B: OK.
A: How much is it per night?
B: 2100 rubles.
A: And do you have Wi-Fi?
B: No, we don't have Wi-Fi.
A: All right, thanks.

SECTION 3: GETTING TO KNOW EACH OTHER

Chapter 11: Nearest and Dearest

У тебя большая семья?

Congratulations! If you reached out to this section – you are able to say quite a lot in Russian. This component is dedicated not to the topics of ultimate survival like eating, shopping or finding a place to stay. Here we will go over some topics that you talk about everyday: people, their families, characters and appearance... It's surely the most exciting part!

In this chapter you will get to know how to learn about people's families and how to tell about yours, e.g. how many brothers or sisters you have, what age they are, etc. You will also learn how to call all family members in Russian. Family matters much to every person, and when you come to Russia you'll definitely appreciate the significance that Russian people attach to the family ties. Here is a new portion of words and expressions that will help you to have a meaty conversation about families.

Family vocabulary and phrases

Do you have any siblings?	У тебя́ есть бра́тья и́ли сёстры?
I have 2 brothers (sisters).	У меня́ два бра́та (две сестры́).
Brother	брат
Sister	сестра́
Parents	роди́тели
Mom	ма́ма
Dad	па́па
Mother	мать
Father	оте́ц
grandpa	де́душка
grandma	ба́бушка
cousin (female/male)	кузен / кузи́на
husband	муж
wife	жена́
son	сын
daughter	дочь
uncle	дя́дя
aunt	тётя
Pet	пито́мец
Dog	соба́ка

Cat (female/male)	ко́шка / кот
Older than	ста́рше чем
Younger than	мла́дше чем
Big brother/ big sister	ста́рший брат / ста́ршая сестра́
Little brother / little sister	мла́дший брат / мла́дшая сестра́

Note that talking about what we have we use the expression *У меня (есть)* from Chapter 8 or *У меня нет* from Chapter 9 of this book. Feel free to come back a little bit and look up some points.

If you want to say *I have a big brother*, you should say *У меня (есть) старший брат*.

But if you want to say that somebody is older or younger than you, you should say, e.g.

Мой брат *старше, чем я*. Моя сестра *младше, чем я*. Мой кот *старше, чем моя собака*. etc. It's convenient for you that the word after the preposition *чем* is in the Nominative case.

Also mind that Russian *дядя* and *тётя* are also used by children to refer to any man or woman. So don't get surprised if you are called *дядя* in the street, people don't think you are their relative!

Possessive Pronouns

You have also noticed words *мой, моя* in the examples above. These are possessive pronouns telling about what people or things belong to. Using Possessive Pronouns in Russian you should take into account the gender and the number of the noun that follows the possessive pronoun (except *his/her* – we look only at the gender of the person to whom belongs the object).

English Pronoun	Female / Masculine forms	Plural form
My	мой / моя́	мои́
Your (singular)	твой / твоя́	твои́
Your (plural and formal)	ваш / ва́ша	ва́ши
His / Her	его́ / её	его́ / её
Our	наш / на́ша	на́ши
Their	их	их

E.g. My mum = моя мама
My siblings = мои братья и сёстры (there's no Russian word for English *siblings*)
Our grandma = наша бабушка
Their pet = их питомец

Show Your Performance!

Match the English word with the corresponding Russian word:

1. Brother	a. ба́бушка
2. Sister	b. муж
3. Mom	c. жена́
4. Dad	d. сын
5. grandpa	e. дочь
6. grandma	f. кузен
7. cousin (male)	g. брат
8. husband	h. сестра́
9. wife	i. ма́ма
10. son	j. па́па
11. daughter	k. де́душка

Put a suitable possessive pronoun instead of a personal pronoun:

1. (Я) _____ братья старше, чем я. (My brothers are older than me).

2. (Он) _____ сестра младще, чем (я) брат. (His sister is younger than my brother).

3. (Мы) _____ бабушка младше, чем (мы) дедушка. (Our grandma is younger than our granddad)

4. (Ты) _____ родители любят ездить в Италию? (Do your parents like to go to Italy)

5. (Они) _____ дочь любит мороженое? (Does their daughter like ice-cream?)

Read it aloud. Guess the meaning of new words. Then write about your own family.

Меня́ зову́т Джон. Мне 23. У меня́ есть мла́дшая сестра́. Ей 15 лет, и её зову́т Алёна. Она́ лю́бит макаро́ны с сы́ром. У неё есть ко́шка, кото́рую зову́т Му́рка. Мою́ ма́му зову́т Еле́на, а моего́ па́пу – Евге́ний. Мы е́здили в Испа́нию в ма́е. У меня́ 2 кузе́на и 1 кузи́на. У неё есть муж и дво́е дете́й. Их зову́т Са́ша и Па́ша. Ещё у мое́й кузи́ны есть соба́ка. У нас есть ба́бушка и де́душка, кото́рые живу́т в Ту́ле.

Chapter 11: Check Yourself

Match the English word with the corresponding Russian word:

1.	Brother	g. брат
2.	Sister	h. сестра
3.	Mom	i. мама
4.	Dad	j. папа
5.	grandpa	k. дедушка
6.	grandma	a. бабушка
7.	cousin (male)	f. кузен
8.	husband	b. муж
9.	wife	c. жена́
10.	son	d. сын
11.	daughter	e. дочь

Put a suitable possessive pronoun instead of a personal pronoun:

1. **Мои** бра́тья ста́рше, чем я. (My brothers are older than me).

2. **Его́** сестра́ мла́дше, чем **мой** брат. (His sister is younger than my brother).

3. **На́ша** ба́бушка мла́дше, чем **наш** де́душка. (Our grandma is younger than our granddad).

4. **Твои́** роди́тели лю́бят е́здить в Ита́лию? (Do your parents like to go to Italy?)

5. **Их** дочь лю́бит моро́женое? (Does their daughter like ice-cream?)

Read it aloud. Guess the meaning of new words. Then write about your own family.

My name is John. I'm 23. I have a younger sister. She's 15 years old and her name is Alyona. She loves macaroni and cheese. She has a (female) cat, its name is Murka. My mother's name is Elena, and my dad's - Eugene. We went (by transport) to Spain in May. I have two male cousins and one female cousin. She has a husband and two children. Their names are Sasha and Pasha. My cousin also has a dog. We have a granny and a granddad who live in Tula.

Chapter 12: Personality (What's She Like...?)

Какой он? Какая она?

Now that you have got to know about the family of your conversation partner and he or she has done the same, it's natural that you and your partner would ask some descriptive questions about people you've been talking about. What are these people like? What do they look like? What about their character? You are making friends with a person form another culture, and it's fantastic how much you can get closer when you learn something special about their family, friends or pets. In this chapter there is a bunch of functional expressions and words aimed to assist you to render the world around you.

Descriptional Phrases

What's he like?	Какой он?
What's she like?	Какая она́?
He is.../She is ...	Он .../Она́ ...
I am...	Я ...
What color is his/her hair?	Како́го цве́та его́ / её во́лосы?
His/her hair is....	Его́ / её во́лосы ....
Does she have long hair?	У неё дли́нные во́лосы?
He has short hair.	У него́ коро́ткие во́лосы.
blonde	блонди́н m / блонди́нка f
brunette	брюне́т m/ брюне́тка f
red-haired	ры́жий m/ ры́жая f

As you see, there's no verb in the phrases of this type.
E.g. Какой он? Он блондин. = What's he like? He is blonde.
Какая она? Она брюнетка. = What's she like? She is brunette.

Appearance Adjectives

tall	высо́кий m/ высо́кая f
short	ни́зкий m/ ни́зкая f
fat	то́лстый m/ то́лстая f
thin	худо́й m/ худа́я f
pretty = handsome	краси́вый m/ краси́вая f
beautiful	прекра́сный m/ прекра́сная f
cute	симпати́чный m/ симпати́чная f

hair	во́лосы *pl*
short (length)	коро́ткий *m*/ коро́ткая *f* /коро́ткие *pl*
long	дли́нный *m*/ дли́нная/ дли́нные *pl*
big	большо́й *m*/большая *f*
small	ма́ленький *m*/ ма́ленькая *f*
strong	си́льный *m*/си́льная *f*
ugly	уро́дливый *m*/ уро́дливая *f*
old	ста́рый *m*/ ста́рая *f*
young	молодо́й *m*/ молода́я *f*

E.g. She is tall. = Она высок**ая**.

Max is young and handsome. = Макс молод**о́й** и красив**ый**.

She's got long hair. = У неё дли́нн**ые** во́лосы.

The Gender of Adjectives

Have you noticed that in the Nominative case masculine adjectives usually end with -ий -ый -ой whereas feminine adjectives end with -ая ? The neutral ones end with -ое. And, finally, adjectives in the plural form end with -ие -ые. Learn it by heart.

Remember this proverb:

> До́брое сло́во и ко́шке прия́тно.

It literally means *Even a cat appreciates kind words.*

Find an adjective in the proverb. What is its gender? Can you draw a conclusion about the gender of the Noun?

The correct answer: **до́брое** is an adjective in the neuter gender; the word **сло́во** is also neuter.

The bottom line: the gender of a Noun is permanent, but the gender of an Adjective is affected by the Noun and can always change. If we don't know the gender of some Noun, we can judge about it having a look at the ending of the adjective relating to this Noun.

Characteristic Adjecctives

These adjectives will help you describe the personality of your near and dear. Since you know how to form the feminine and neuter forms of the adjectives, do it with the following ones given in the masculine form.

kind	до́брый
mean	злой
funny (hilarious)	весёлый, заба́вный
easy-going	общи́тельный
shy	скро́мный
brave	хра́брый
cowardly	трусли́вый

By the way, *злой* is the only one-syllable adjective in the Russian language!

Show Your Performance!

Read and translate the phrases, guess the gender of the Nouns:

Зелёная трава́, высо́кая гора́, чёрный блокно́т, ора́нжевое со́лнце, ни́зкий ма́льчик, то́лстый мужчи́на, худа́я же́нщина, заба́вный актёр, трусли́вая соба́ка, до́брый челове́к, ма́ленький ребёнок, симпати́чная де́вушка, прекра́сная кни́га.

Read aloud and translate the sentences into Englsih:

1. Кака́я она́?
2. Она́ высо́кая, краси́вая и молода́я.
3. Каки́е у неё во́лосы?
4. Она́ блонди́нка, и у неё дли́нные во́лосы.
5. Како́й он?
6. У него́ коро́ткие во́лосы?
7. Да, у него́ коро́ткие чёрные во́лосы.
8. Она́ общи́тельная и заба́вная.
9. Твой брат хра́брый?
10. Моя́ ма́ма до́брая и скро́мная.

Emotion Vocabulary

There are also lots of temporary qualities that are aimed to describe our inner state. Have a look at the list of emotion vocabulary. As usual, no verb is needed in a sentence.

E.g. Я счастливый. = I am happy.

How do you feel?	Как ты себя чу́вствуешь?
I feel...	Я ...
Happy	Счастлив / счастли́ва
Sad	Гру́стный / весёлый
Tired	Уста́л / уста́ла
Excited	Волну́юсь
Angry	Злой / зла́я
Nervous	Не́рвный / не́рвная
Calm	Споко́йный / споко́йная
Busy	За́нят / занята́
Brave	Мне стра́шно
Bored	Мне ску́чно

*The phrases starting with *мне* (мне скучно, мне страшно) don't recqiure the use of the pronoun «я»..

Remember these phrases:

I feel fine. = Я чу́вствую себя́ хорошо́.
I feel badly. = Я чу́вствую себя́ пло́хо.

Show Your Performance!

Match the English word with the corresponding Russian word:

1. Funny	a. счастливый
2. Young	b. волнуюсь
3. Happy	c. спокойный
4. Sad	d. занят
5. Tired	e. весёлый
6. Excited	f. грустный
7. Kind	g. добрый

8. Nervous	h. храбрый
9. Calm	i. мне скучно
10. Busy	j. молодой
11. Brave	k. устал
12. Bored	l. нервный

Chapter 12: Check Yourself

Read and translate the phrases, guess the gender of the Nouns:

Зелёная трава́ – green grass (f), высо́кая гора́ – a high mountain (f), чёрный блокно́т a black notepad (m), ора́нжевое со́лнце the orange sun (m), ни́зкий ма́льчик - a short boy (m), то́лстый мужчи́на – a fat man (m), худа́я же́нщина - a thin woman (f), заба́вный актёр – a funny actor (m), трусли́вая соба́ка – a cowardly dog (f), до́брый челове́к - a kind person (m), ма́ленький ребёнок – a little child (m), симпати́чная де́вушка – a cute lady (f), прекра́сная кни́га – a beautiful book (f).

Read aloud and translate the sentences into Englsih:

1. Какая она́? = What's she like?
2. Она высокая, красивая и молодая. = She's tall, pretty and young.
3. Какие у неё волосы? = What hair does she have?
4. Она́ блонди́нка, и у неё дли́нные во́лосы. = She is blonde, and she has long hair.
5. Какой он? = What's he like?
6. У него короткие волосы? = Is his hair short?
7. Да, у него́ коро́ткие чёрные во́лосы. = Yes, he has short black hair.
8. Она общительная и забавная. = She is easy-going and funny.
9. Твой брат храбрый? = Is your brother brave?
10. Моя ма́ма до́брая и скро́мная. = My mom is kind and shy.

Match the English word with the corresponding Russian word:

1. Funny	e. весёлый
2. Young	j. молодой
3. Happy	a. счастливый
4. Sad	f. грустный
5. Tired	k. устал
6. Excited	b. волнуюсь

7. Kind	g. добрый
8. Nervous	l. нервный
9. Calm	c. спокойный
10. Busy	d. занят
11. Brave	h. храбрый
12. Bored	i. мне скучно

Chapter 13: Professions (Teacher, Lawyer, Scientist!)

Чем ты занима́ешься?

It's very likely that after finding out what your Russian friend's family is like you will be bursting to learn about his or her occupation. Imagine the following situation: your new girl friend looks just like a balley dancer, plus has unbelievably intelligible speech, so you understand every word and want to listen to her infinitely... What phrase are you going to say? Don't panic, keep your shurt on! Just smile and utter peacefully *Чем ты занима́ешься?* She'll instantly reveal her secret.

Take into account that being a part of the Eastern world, the Russian people traditionally doesn't attach so much importance to work and business achievements as, for example, many European cultures. So, don't tell what a successful businessman you are if you weren't asked. Otherwise, people may think that you are arrogant. In this chapter, you will get to know how to have this kind of conversation.

Occupational vocabulary and phrases:

Note that some of the occupations like *бизнесме́н* and *студе́нт / студе́нтка* are loan words from the English language. So, mastering this topic is a piece of cake for you!

What do you do?	Чем ты занима́ешься?
What do you do? (formal, plural)	Чем вы занима́етесь?
Teacher	учи́тель / учи́тельница
Businessman	бизнесме́н
Doctor	врач
Nurse	медсестра́/медбра́т
Lawyer	адвока́т
Writer	писа́тель /писа́тельница
Policeman	полице́йский
Firefighter	пожа́рный
Engineer	инжене́р
Scientist	учёный
Waiter	официа́нт / официа́нтка
Cook	по́вар
Salesperson	продаве́ц / продавщи́ца

Student	студе́нт / студе́нтка

Not all professions in Russian have both masculine and feminine forms. Some activities which traditionally have been performed by men, have remained masculine in the form.

E.g. He's a doctor. = Он врач. She's a doctor. = Она врач.

He's a cook. = Он повар. She's a cook. = Она повар.

Sometimes it's not convenient - not knowing whether a person refers to a man or a woman. But in English it's always like this, therefore if it's your Native language it's not going to be a problem for you.

And remember a Russian proverb:

Делу время, а потехе час. (Devote time to business and an hour to fun)

Show Your Performance!

Match the English word with the corresponding Russian word:

1. Teacher	a. ме́дсестра́/медбра́т
2. Businessman	b. официа́нт / официа́нтка
3. Doctor	c. писа́тель /писа́тельница
4. Nurse	d. учёный
5. Lawyer	e. учи́тель / учи́тельница
6. Writer	f. бизнесме́н
7. Policeman	g. адвока́т
8. Firefighter	h. врач
9. Engineer	i. полице́йский
10. Scientist	j. продаве́ц / продавщи́ца
11. Waiter	k. пожа́рный
12. Cook	l. инжене́р
13. Salesperson	m. по́вар
14. Student	n. студе́нт / студе́нтка

Put the correct form of the word according to the gender:
1. Он _____ (продаве́ц / продавщи́ца).

2. Она _____ (студéнт / студéнтка).
3. Маша _____ (официáнт / официáнтка).
4. Кирилл _____ (мéдсестрá/медбрáт).
5. Я _____ (писáтель /писáтельница). (Answer according to your gender)

Answer the following question about your occupation. Don't forget to answer according to your gender. Look it up in the dictionary if your profession is not listed above.
Чем ты занимаешься?
_____

Chapter 13: Check Yourself

Match the English word with the corresponding Russian word:

1.	Teacher	e. учи́тель / учи́тельница
2.	Businessman	f. бизнесмéн
3.	Doctor	h. врач
4.	Nurse	a. мéдсестрá/медбрáт
5.	Lawyer	g. адвокáт
6.	Writer	c. писáтель /писáтельница
7.	Policeman	i. полицéйский
8.	Firefighter	k. пожáрный
9.	Engineer	l. инженéр
10.	Scientist	d. учёный
11.	Waiter	b. официáнт / официáнтка
12.	Cook	m. пóвар
13.	Salesperson	j. продавéц / продавщи́ца
14.	Student	n. студéнт / студéнтка

Put the correct form of the word according to the gender:
1. Он **продавéц**.
2. Она **студéнтка**.
3. Маша - **официáнтка**.
4. Кирилл - **медбрáт**.
5. Я _____ (писáтель /писáтельница). (Answers may vary)

Chapter 14: Free Time and Hobbies

Чем ты любишь заниматься?

Every person in the world has their interests and hobbies, and this topic is so universal that you can apply it in a conversation with either a 5 year-old child or a 100 year-old babushka! Either of them will eagerly tell you that they love playing the balalaika or they can't live without doing knitting or whatever! You simply MUST be able to ask and answer questions about people's personal habits, hobbies and interests. Who knows, may be you'll find a person who enjoys playing the same videogames or listening to the same music with you?

Consider that many people in Russia tend to simply spend their free time with their friends having fun, chatting and discussing problems. And some people in fact suffer from lack of time to do their hobbies.

In this chapter you will discover handy phrases relating to hobbies and the conjugation of the verb *жить* so that you can talk about where you live. We'll also discuss the use of the last case of the Russian language – the Prepositional case.

Hobbies Vocabulary

What do you like doing? (formal)	Что ты любишь делать?
What do you like doing? (informal)	Что вы любите делать?
I like …	Мне нравится … *singular*
	Мне нравятся … *plural*
I don't like …	Мне не нравится… *singular*
	Мне не нравятся … *plural*
free time	свободное время
to do sports	заниматься спортом
to play videogames	играть в видеоигры
to travel	путешествовать
to read	читать
to go to the movies	ходить в кино
to go to the beach	ходить на пляж
to watch TV	смотреть телевизор
to watch sports TV programmes	смотреть спортивные программы
to listen to music	слушать музыку
to play the… (piano, guitar, violin)	играть на …(пианино, гитаре,

	скри́пке)
to ski / skate	ката́ться на лы́жах / конька́х
to spend time with friends	проводи́ть вре́мя с друзья́ми

The construction *Мне нра́вится...* as well as the construction *Я люблю́...* requires the infinitive form of the verb or a Noun (even if there is a preceding adjective).

E.g. Мне нра́вится **слу́шать** класси́ческую му́зыку. = I like listening to classical music.

Мне нра́вится <u>класси́ческая **му́зыка**</u>. = I like classical music.

What if you need to say to someone where you live? It is straightforwardly associated with the traveling issue, so to learn how to conjugate the verb *жить* (to live) is essential.

	жить (to live)	в чём? (in what?) на чём? (on what?)
I live	я живу́	в го́роде (in the city)
You live	ты живёшь	в дере́вне (in the country)
He/She/It lives	Он/она́ живёт	в Ло́ндоне (in London)
We live	мы живём	в Москве́ (in Moscow)
You guys live (or formal)	вы живёте	в Нью-Йо́рке (in NY)
They live	они́ живу́т	в Пари́же (in Paris)
(He) lived, (she) lived, (we, they) lived	жил, жила́, жи́ли	на остро́ве (on an island)

The Nouns from the last column are given in the <u>Prepositional Case</u>. It is always used with a preposition and is used to denote a place, a person or a thing that is an object of speech and thought.

E.g. The cafe is on the roof. = Кафе́ <u>на</u> <u>кры́ше</u>.

I'm thinking about a big city. = Я ду́маю <u>о</u> <u>большо́м</u> <u>го́роде</u>.

What is the typical ending of this case? Right, the ending -e.

Show Your Performance!

Match the Englsih phrase to the corresponding phrase in Russian:

1. spend time with friends	a. играть в видеоигры
2. to do sports	b. играть на гитаре
3. to play videogames	c. смотреть телевизор
4. to travel	d. слу́шать му́зыку
5. to read	e. проводить вре́мя с друзья́ми
6. to go to the movies	f. занима́ться спо́ртом
7. to watch TV	g. читать
8. to listen to music	h. путеше́ствовать
9. to play the guitar	i. ходить в кино

Choose the correct answer:

1. I live in the country.
a. Я живу в городе.------------------b. Ты живешь в деревне.
c. Я живу в деревне.----------------d. Ты живу в городе.

2. Do you live in London?
a. Ты живёт в Лондоне? --------------------b. Он живёт в Лондоне?
c. Мы живём в Лондоне? --------------------d. Ты живёшь в Лондоне?

3. Мы живем на большом острове.
a. We live on a big island.------------------- b. We live on a small island.
c. He lives on a big island.-------------------d. He lives on a small island

4. Вы живёте в Париже?
a. Do we live in Paris?-------------------- b. Do you live in Paris?
c. Does he live in Paris?------------------d. Does she live in Paris?

Chapter 14: Check Yourself

Match the Englsih phrase to the corresponding phrase in Russian:

10. spend time with friends	a. играть в видеоигры
11. to do sports	b. играть на гитаре
12. to play videogames	c. смотреть телевизор
13. to travel	d. слу́шать му́зыку
14. to read	e. проводить вре́мя с друзья́ми

15. to go to the movies	f. заниматься спортом
16. to watch TV	g. читать
17. to listen to music	h. путешествовать
18. to play the guitar	i. ходить в кино

Choose the correct answer:

1. I live in the country.
c. Я живу в деревне.

2. Do you live in London?
d. Ты живёшь в Лондоне?

3. Мы живем на большом острове.
a. We live on a big island.

4. Вы живёте в Париже?
b. Do you live in Paris?

SECTION 4: GRAMMAR SCHOOL

Grammar Challenges for Russian Learners

Cases of the Russian Language

One of the most diverse grammar categories in the Russian language, which is a matter immense of difficulties for language learners, is, of course, the category of Case. There are 6 Russian cases all in all, and each of them provides different endings for the Nouns. There are some fine points under each case listed below, so that you could find a purpose of your utterance and put the right ending to the Noun you need to decline. We recommend you become skilled at all the declensions of the Russian cases. We suggest learning the declension of one word a day, so that later on you were able to use it quickly and automatically. Revise this material every day, and the results will not keep you waiting.

Nominative Case

Nominative is the main and basic case of the Russian language. We employ it in language structures that answer the questions *what? who?* If the Noun is the subject of a sentence – its case is usually Nominative.

Gender	Singular	Ending	Plural	Ending
Masculine	диван музей корабль	-ø	диваны музеи корабли	-ы -и
Neuter	кресло здание	-о -е	кресла здания	-а -я
Feminine	газета пекарня мать	-а -я -ø	газеты пекарни матери	-ы -и

Genitive Case

Genitive Case is used in constructions answering the questions *whom? whose?* There are several major types of conditions when we use this case:

- to indicate possession, like the English **'s**, e.g. книга студент**а** (student's book), дом родител**ей** (parents' house)
- to indicate the "**of**" relationship, e.g. чашка ча**я** (a cup of tea), портрет Дориан**а** Гре**я** (the picture of Dorian Grey), собрание сочинен**ий** (a collection of works)

- to denote that something is missing and that there is none of some objects, e.g. нет ри**са** (there's no rice), нет ид**ей** (there are no ideas), нет мес**та** (there's no place)
- to specify some numbers, e. g. 1000 рубл**ей** (1000 Rubles), 200 доллар**ов** (200 dollars), 3 стака**на** (3 glasses)
- the pronouns we use to say *(У меня) есть* (I have... There is ...) are the genitive case of the personal pronouns *я, ты, он* etc. Here they are: я – *меня*, ты – *тебя*, он – *(н)его*, она – *(н)её*, оно – *(н)его*, мы – *нас*, они – *(н)их*. E.g. Я <u>тебя</u> люблю (I love you), он любит <u>её</u> (he loves her), etc.

Gender	Nominative Singular	Genitive Singular	Ending	Genitive Plural	Ending
Masculine	стол студент музей корабль писатель	стола студента музея корабля писателя	-а -я	столов студентов музеев кораблей писателей	-ов -ев -ей
Neuter	окно здание	окна здания	-а -я	окон зданий	-∅
Feminine	газета неделя история	газеты недели истории	-ы -и	газет недель историй	-∅
	тетрадь	тетради	-и	тетрадей	-ей

Dative Case

The Dative Case is used in the following scenarios:

- something is done **to** or **for** somebody, e.g. сказать <u>Ивану</u> (to give to Ivan), читать <u>ребёнку</u> (to read to a child), не верить <u>газетам</u> (not to believe newspapers), помогать <u>людям</u> (to help people).

- something is given to somebody (*давать* = to give), e.g. Он дал <u>Кате</u> свою тетрадь (He gave <u>Kate</u> his notebook); Учитель даёт <u>студентам</u> время на размышление (The teacher gives the <u>students</u> some time to think).
- somebody goes **towards** some place or to someone's place, e.g. Я еду <u>к морю</u> (I'm driving towards the sea); Она идёт <u>к подруге</u> (She's going to her friend's place); Мы направились <u>к дому</u> (We headed towards the house).
- somebody likes something (*нравиться* = to like). The personal pronouns in the Dative case acquire the following forms: я – *мне*, ты – *тебе*, он – *ему*, она – *ей*, оно – *ему*, мы – *нам*, они – *нам*. E.g. <u>Мне</u> нравится ходить на пляж. (I like going to the beach). <u>Ей</u> нравятся бананы. (She likes apples).
- somebody is cold, hot etc., so we express somebody's emotional or physical state, e.g. <u>Наташе</u> холодно. (Literally: to Natasha it's cold); <u>Футболистам</u> жарко (The football players are cold); <u>Нам</u> страшно. (We are scared).
- talking about age, e.g. <u>Мне</u> 30 лет (Literally: to me there are 30 years); <u>ей</u> 18 лет (she's 18 years old) etc.
-

Gender	Nominative Singular	Dative Singular	Ending	Dative Plural	Ending
Masculine	стол студент музей корабль писатель	столу студенту музею кораблю писателю	-у -ю	столам студентам музеям кораблям писателям	-ам -ям
Neuter	окно здание	окну зданию	-у -ю	окнам зданиям	-ам -ям
Feminine	газета неделя история	газете неделе истории	-е -и	газетам неделям историям	-ам -ям

	тетрадь	тетради	-и	тетрадям	-ям

Instrumental Case

The Instrumental case is applied to point up the notion "by", "with the help of", "by means of".

We use it in the following situations:

- denoting an instrument of the action, e.g. Я пишу <u>ручк**ой**</u> (I'm writing with a pen). Захар рубит дерево <u>топор**ом**</u>. (Zakhar is cutting a tree with an axe)
- expressing the idea of addition, accompaniment, meaning "with", "together", e.g. чай <u>с лимон**ом**</u> (tea with lemon); Лена гуляет <u>с друзь**ями**</u> (Lena is walking with friends), Анна <u>с Антон**ом**</u> идут в магазин (Anna and Anton are going to a shop). The personal pronouns in the Instrumental case take the following shape: я – *мной*, ты – *тобой*, он – (*н*)*им*, она – (*н*)*ей*, оно – (*н*)*им*, мы – *нами*, они – (*н*)*ими*. E.g. Ты пойдёшь со <u>мной</u> или с <u>ними</u>? (Will you go with me or with them?).
- talking about seasons and parts of the day, answering the question *when?* e.g. зим**ой** (in winter), лет**ом** (in summer), дн**ём** (in the daytime), ночь**ю** (at night) etc.
- after some prepositions: *перед* (in front of), *на* (on), *под* (under) *над* (over), *за* (behind), e.g. за угл**ом** (around = behind the corner), под стол**ом** (under the table), перед здани**ями** (in front of the buildings)

Gender	Nominative Singular	Instrumental Singular	Ending	Instrumental Plural	Ending
Masculine	стол студент музей корабль писатель	столом студентом музеем кораблём писателем	-ом -ем (-ём)	столами студентами музеями кораблями писателями	-ами -ями
Neuter	окно здание	окном зданием	-ом -ем	окнами зданиями	-ами -ями

	газета неделя история	газетой неделей историей	-ой -ей	газетами неделями историями	-ами -ями
Feminine	тетрадь	тетрадью	-ю	тетрадями	-ями

Prepositional Case

The Prepositional case is used after some prepositions: *о, об* (about), *в* (in, inside), *на* (at, on), e.g. картинки <u>в журнал**ах**</u> (pictures in the magazines); капли <u>на стекл**е**</u> (drops on the glass); книга <u>о пират**ах**</u> (a book about pirates).

It creates the following forms of the personal pronouns: я – *мне*, ты – *тебе*, он – *нём*, она – н*ей*, оно – *нём*, мы – *нас*, они – *них*. E.g. Ты думаешь <u>о них</u>? (Are you thinking about them?).

Gender	Nominative Singular	Prepositional Singular	Ending	Prepositional Plural	Ending
Masculine	стол студент музей корабль писатель	столе студенте музее корабле писателе	-е	столах студентах музеях кораблях писателях	-ах -ях
Neuter	окно здание	окне здании	-е -и	окнах зданиях	-ах -ях
Feminine	газета неделя история	газете неделе истории	-е -и	газетах неделях историях	-ах -ях
	тетрадь	тетради	-и	тетрадях	-ях

BONUS SECTION

Top 50 Russian Nouns

1. челове́к *m* (man, person)
2. год *m* (year)
3. вре́мя *n* (time)
4. рука́ *f* (hand)
5. де́ло *n* (business, affair, matter)
6. раз *m* (time, once, since)
7. глаз *m* (eye; sight)
8. жизнь *f* (life)
9. день *m* (day)
10. голова́ *f* (head, mind, brains)
11. друг *m* (friend)
12. дом *m* (house, home)
13. сло́во *n* (word)
14. ме́сто *n* (place; seat)
15. лицо́ *n* (face; person)
16. сторона́ *f* (side, party)
17. нога́ *f* (foot, leg)
18. дверь *f* (door)
19. рабо́та *f* (work, job)
20. земля́ *f* (earth, land, soil)
21. коне́ц *m* (end, distance)
22. час *m* (hour, time)
23. го́лос *m* (voice)
24. го́род *m* (town, city)
25. вода́ *f* (water)
26. стол *m* (table, desk; board)
27. ребёнок *m* (child, kid, infant)
28. си́ла *f* (strength, force)
29. оте́ц *m* (father)
30. же́нщина *f* (woman)
31. маши́на *f* (car, machine, engine)
32. слу́чай *m* (case, occasion, incident)
33. ночь *f* (night)
34. мир *m* (world)
35. вид *m* (appearance, look, view)
36. ряд *m* (row, line)
37. нача́ло *n* (beginning, origin, source)
38. вопро́с *m* (question, matter, problem)

39. война́ *f* (war)
40. де́ньги *plural* (money)
41. мину́та *f* (minute, moment)
42. жена́ *f* (wife)
43. пра́вда *f* (truth)
44. страна́ *f* (country)
45. свет *m* (light; world)
46. мать *f* (mother)
47. това́рищ *m* (comrade, friend)
48. доро́га *f* (road, way, journey)
49. окно́ *n* (window, windowsill)
50. ко́мната *f* (a room)

Top 50 Russian Verbs

1. быть (to be, have)
2. сказа́ть (to say, speak)
3. мочь (to be able)
4. говори́ть (to say, tell, speak)
5. знать (to know, be aware)
6. стать (to become, begin, come)
7. есть (to eat, to be)
8. хоте́ть (to want, like)
9. ви́деть (to see)
10. идти́ (to go, come)
11. стоя́ть (to stand, be, stand up)
12. ду́мать (to think)
13. спроси́ть (to ask)
14. жить (to live)
15. смотре́ть (to look, watch, see)
16. сиде́ть (to sit)
17. поня́ть (to understand; realize)
18. име́ть (to have, own)
19. де́лать (to do, make)
20. взять (to take)
21. сде́лать (to do, make, finish)
22. понима́ть (to understand)
23. каза́ться (to seem, appear)
24. дава́ть (to give; let, allow)
25. пойти́ (to go)

26. уви́деть (to see)
27. оста́ться (to remain, stay)
28. вы́йти (to go out, come out, appear)
29. дать (to give)
30. рабо́тать (to work)
31. люби́ть (to love)
32. оказа́ться (to find oneself, turn out)
33. отве́тить (to answer, reply)
34. поду́мать (to think)
35. зна́чить (to mean, signify)
36. посмотре́ть (to take a look, watch, inspect)
37. ждать (to wait)
38. лежа́ть (to lie, be situated)
39. найти́ to find, (to discover, consider)
40. писа́ть (to write)
41. реши́ть (to decide, solve)
42. верну́ться (to return)
43. счита́ть (to count, consider)
44. по́мнить (to remember)
45. получи́ть (to receive, get, obtain)
46. ходи́ть (to go, walk)
47. быва́ть (to be, visit, happen)
48. прийти́ (to come, arrive)
49. узна́ть (to know, learn, recognize)
50. заме́тить (to notice, observe)

Top 50 Russian Adjectives

1. большо́й (big)
2. интере́сный (interesting)
3. ка́ждый (every)
4. стра́нный (strange)
5. тру́дный (difficult)
6. смешно́й (funny)
7. весёлый (cheerful)
8. лёгкий (light)
9. ва́жный (important)
10. ра́вный (equal)
11. молодо́й (young)
12. твёрдый (firm, hard)

13. хоро́ший (good)
14. больно́й (ill, sick)
15. одина́ковый (equal)
16. бе́дный (poor)
17. возмо́жный (possible)
18. со́бственный (one's own)
19. кра́сный (red)
20. гря́зный (dirty)
21. просто́й (simple)
22. споко́йный (calm)
23. гру́стный (sad)
24. пусто́й (empty)
25. свобо́дный (free)
26. ра́нний (early)
27. сла́дкий (sweet)
28. до́брый (kind)
29. ру́сский (Russian)
30. то́лстый (thick)
31. счастли́вый (happy)
32. плохо́й (bad)
33. серьёзный (serious)
34. ста́рый (old)
35. настоя́щий (real, natural)
36. но́вый (new)
37. краси́вый (beautiful)
38. бе́лый (white)
39. не́который (some)
40. жа́ркий (hot)
41. дорого́й (expensive)
42. я́сный (clear)
43. стра́шный (old)
44. после́дний (last)
45. бы́стрый (fast)
46. ра́зный (different)
47. пра́вый (right)
48. це́лый (whole)
49. си́льный (strong)
50. холо́дный (cold)

*All adjectives are given in the masculine singular of the Nominative case.

Afterword

Time to Launch Out On Your Own Voyage of Discovery!

Congratulations! You traveled a long way and achieved lots of goals. Each chapter was a hard nut to crack. It was not painless, but, as they say, *всё хорошо, что хорошо кончается* (all is well that ends well). So, your crash course has come to a close.

Apply your knowledge and language skills in any possible and impossible way! Even if you have no one to talk to in Russian, talk to your hamster, or to your refrigerator, or to a lamppost at the worst! Foreign language is like sports: if you don't use it, you lose it. You might effortlessly lose your perfect "Russian sixpack" you've made by now if you don't practice.

Hopefully, you are a realist and you don't think you are the expert on the Pushkin's language! As you remember from the foreword, the basis that you should have grasped by this moment is a raft that can help you float on the water and not to go under. This raft needs to be taken care of, and, who knows, some day you may realize that it became a huge vessel! Have a grip on the situation, learn new words every day, read books in Russian, listen to Russian songs, watch Russian movies and don't worry about how you appear to others! It's better sometimes to look silly mastering a trade or a skill, than avoid the discomfort in fear of getting into an embarrassing situation. If you don't know how to express your thought, apply any potential supports, like pantomime, gestures, context clues, paraphrasing, and you will ultimately hit upon the answer.

I wish you every success!

До свидания!

Dagny Taggart

Learn Any Language 300% FASTER

>> Get Full Online Language Courses With Audio Lessons <<

Would you like to learn a new language before you start your trip? I think that's a great idea. Now, why don't you do it 300% *FASTER*?

I've partnered with the most revolutionary language teachers to bring you the very language online courses I've ever seen. It's a mind-blowing program specifically created for language hackers such as ourselves. It will allow you learn ANY language, from French to Chinese, 3x faster, straight from the comfort of your own home, office, or wherever you may be. It's like having an unfair advantage!

You can choose from a wide variety of languages, such as French, Spanish, Italian, German, Chinese, Portuguese, and A TON more.

Each Online Course consists of:

+ 91 Built-In Lessons
+ 33 Interactive Audio Lessons
+ 24/7 Support to Keep You Going

The program is extremely engaging, fun, and easy-going. You won't even notice you are learning a complex foreign language from scratch. And before you realize it, by the time you go through all the lessons you will officially become a truly solid speaker.

Old classrooms are a thing of the past. It's time for a revolution.

If you'd like to go the extra mile, the click the button below or follow the link, and let the revolution begin

>> http://bitly.com/foreign-language-courses <<

CHECK OUT THE COURSE »

PS: Can I Ask You a Quick Favor?

If you liked the book, please leave a nice review on Amazon! I'd absolutely love to hear your feedback. Every time I read your reviews... you make me smile. I'd be immensely thankful if you go to Amazon now, and write down a quick line sharing with me your experience. I personally read ALL the reviews there, and I'm thrilled to hear your feedback and honest motivation. It's what keeps me going, and helps me improve everyday =)

Please go Amazon now and drop a quick review sharing your experience!

***

THANKS!

***

ONCE YOU'RE BACK,
FLIP THE PAGE!
BONUS CHAPTER AHEAD
=)

Preview Of "Learn Spanish In 7 DAYS! - The Ultimate Crash Course To Learn The Basics of the Spanish Language In No Time"

Are You ready? It's Time To Learn Spanish!

Most people are daunted by the idea of learning a language. They think it's impossible, even unfathomable. I remember as a junior in high school, watching footage of Jackie O giving a speech in French. I was so impressed and inspired by the ease at which she spoke this other language of which I could not understand one single word.

At that moment, I knew I had to learn at least one foreign language. I started with Spanish, later took on Mandarin, and most recently have started learning Portuguese. No matter how challenging and unattainable it may seem, millions of people have done it. You do NOT have to be a genius to learn another language. You DO have to be willing to take risks and make mistakes, sometimes even make a fool of yourself, be dedicated, and of course, practice, practice, practice!

This book will only provide you with the basics in order to get started learning the Spanish language. It is geared towards those who are planning to travel to a Spanish-speaking country and covers many common scenarios you may find yourself in so feel free to skip around to the topic that is most prudent to you at the moment. It is also focused on the Spanish of Latin America rather than Spain. Keep in mind, every Spanish-speaking country has some language details specific to them so it would be essential to do some research on the specific country or countries that you will visit.

I will now list some tips that I have found useful and should be very helpful to you in your journey of learning Spanish. I don't wish you luck because that will not get you anywhere- reading this book, dedicating yourself, and taking some risks will!

Important note

Due to the nature of this book (it contains charts, graphs, and so on), you will better your reading experience by setting your device on *LANDSCAPE* mode! (In case you're using an electronic device like Kindle).

Language Tips

Tip #1 - Keep an Open Mind

It may seem obvious but you must understand that languages are very different from each other. You cannot expect them to translate word for word. *'There is a black dog'* will not translate word for word with the same word order in Spanish. You have to get used to the idea of translating WHOLE ideas. So don't find yourself saying, *"Why is everything backwards in Spanish?"* because it may seem that way many times. Keep your mind open to the many differences that you will find in the language that go far beyond just the words.

Tip #2 - Take Risks

Be fearless. Talk to as many people as you can. The more practice you get the better and don't worry about looking like a fool when you say, *"I am pregnant"* rather than *"I am embarrassed,"* which as you will find out can be a common mistake. If anyone is laughing remember they are not laughing at you. Just laugh with them, move on, and LEARN from it, which brings us to our next tip.

Tip #3 - Learn from your Mistakes

It doesn't help to get down because you made one more mistake when trying to order at a restaurant, take a taxi, or just in a friendly conversation. Making mistakes is a HUGE part of learning a language. You have to put yourself out there as we said and be willing to make tons of mistakes! Why? Because what can you do with mistakes. You can LEARN from them. If you never make a mistake, you probably are not learning as much as you could. So every time you mess up when trying to communicate, learn from it, move on, and keep your head up!

Tip #4 - Immerse yourself in the language

If you're not yet able to go to a Spanish-speaking country, try to pretend that you are. Surround yourself with Spanish. Listen to music in Spanish, watch movies, TV shows, in Spanish. Play games on your phone, computer, etc. in Spanish. Another great idea is to actually put your phone, computer, tablet and/or other electronic devices in Spanish. It can be frustrating at first but in the end this exposure will definitely pay off.

Tip #5 - Start Thinking in Spanish

I remember being a senior in high school and working as a lifeguard at a fairly deserted pool. While I was sitting and staring at the empty waters, I would speak to myself or think to myself (to not seem so crazy) in Spanish. I would describe my surroundings, talk about what I had done and what I was going to do, etc. While I was riding my bike, I would do the same thing. During any activity when you don't need to talk or think about anything else, keep your brain constantly going in Spanish to get even more practice in the language. So get ready to turn off the English and jumpstart your Spanish brain!

Tip #6 - Label your Surroundings/Use Flashcards

When I started to learn Portuguese, I bought an excellent book that included stickers so that you could label your surroundings. So I had stickers all over my parents' house from the kitchen to the bathroom that labeled the door, the dishes, furniture, parts of the house, etc. It was a great, constant reminder of how to say these objects in another language. You can just make your own labels and stick them all over the house and hope it doesn't bother your family or housemates too much!

Tip #7 - Use Context clues, visuals, gestures, expressions, etc.

If you don't understand a word that you have heard or read, look or listen to the surrounding words and the situation to help you. If you are in a restaurant and your friend says, "I am going to ??? a sandwich." You can take a guess that she said *order* or *eat* but you don't have to understand every word in order to understand the general meaning. When you are in a conversation use gestures, expressions, and things around you to help communicate your meaning. Teaching English as a second language to young learners taught me this. If you act everything out, you are more likely to get your point across. If you need to say the word *bird* and you don't know how you can start flapping your arms and chirping and then you will get your point across and possibly learn how to say *bird*. It may seem ridiculous but as I said, you have to be willing to look silly to learn another language and this greatly helps your language communication and learning.

Tip #8 - Circumlocution

Circumlo... what? This is just a fancy word for describing something when you don't know how to say it. If you are looking to buy an umbrella and don't know how to say it, what can you do? You can describe it using words you know. You can say, it is something used for the rain that opens and closes and then hopefully someone will understand you, help you, and maybe teach you how to say this word. Using circumlocution is excellent language practice and is much better than just giving up when you don't know how to say a word. So keep talking even if you have a limited vocabulary. Say what you can and describe or act out what you can't!

SECTION 1: THE BASICS

Chapter 1: Getting the Pronunciation Down

Below I will break down general Spanish pronunciation for the whole alphabet dividing it into vowels and consonants. One great thing about Spanish is that the letters almost always stay consistent as far as what sound they make. Unlike English in which the vowels can make up to 27 different sounds depending on how they are mixed. Be thankful that you don't have to learn English or at least have already learned English. There are of course some sounds in Spanish that we never make in English and you possibly have never made in your life. So get ready to start moving your mouth and tongue in a new way that may seem strange at first but as I keep saying, practice makes perfect!

The charts on the next page will explain how to say the letter, pronounce it, and if there is an example in an English word of how to say it I put it in the right column.

Vowel Sounds

Vowel	How to say the letter	How to pronounce it in a word	As in...
a	Ah	Ah	T<u>a</u>co
e	Eh	Eh	<u>E</u>gg
i	Ee	Ee	<u>Eas</u>y

o	Oh	Oh	<u>O</u>pen
u	Oo	Oo	B<u>oo</u>k

Consonant Sounds

Consonant	How to say the letter	How to pronounce it in a word	As in…
b	beh	similar to English b	
c	ceh	k after *a, o,* or *u* s after *e* or *i*	<u>c</u>at <u>c</u>ereal
ch	cheh	ch	<u>ch</u>eese
d	deh	a soft d (place your tongue at the back of your upper teeth)	<u>th</u>ree
f	efe	F	<u>f</u>ree
g	geh	h before i or e g before a, o, u	<u>h</u>im <u>g</u>o
h	ache	silent	
j	hota	H	<u>h</u>im
k	kah	K	<u>k</u>araoke
l	ele	like English l with tongue raised to roof of mouth	
ll	eye	Y	<u>y</u>es
m	eme	M	<u>m</u>oney
n	ene	N	<u>n</u>o
ñ	enye	Ny	can<u>y</u>on
p	peh	like English p but you don't aspirate	

Consonants continued

Consonant	How to say the letter	How to pronounce it in a word	As in…

Q	koo	k (q is always followed by u like English)	quilt
R	ere	* at the beginning of a word you must roll your r's by vibrating tongue at roof of mouth * in the middle of a word it sounds like a soft d	
rr	erre	roll your r's as mentioned above	
S	ese	Like English s	sorry
T	teh	a soft English t, the tongue touches the back of the upper teeth	
V	veh	like Spanish b	boots

Consonants continued

Consonant	How to say the letter	How to pronounce it in a word	As in…
w	dobleveh	like English w	water
x	equis	*Between vowels and at the end of a word, it sounds like the English *ks*. *At the beginning of a word, it sounds like the letter *s*.	*box *sorry
y	igriega	like English y	yellow
z	seta	s	six

Note: If you're not sure how to pronounce a word, one thing you can do is type it in *Google translate* then click on the little speaker icon in the bottom left corner to hear the correct pronunciation.

To check out the rest of *"Learn Spanish In 7 DAYS! - The Ultimate Crash Course To Learning The Basics of The Spanish Language In No Time"*, **go to Amazon and look for it right now!**

Ps: You'll find many more books like these under my name, Dagny Taggart. Don't miss them! Here's a short list:

- Learn **Spanish** In 7 Days!
- Learn **French** In 7 Days!
- Learn **German** In 7 Days!
- Learn **Italian** In 7 Days!
- Learn **Portuguese** In 7 Days!

- Learn **Japanese** In 7 Days!
- Learn **Chinese** In 7 Days!

- Learn **Russian** In 7 Days!

- Learn Any Language FAST!

- How to Drop Everything & Travel Around The World

Check Out My Other Books

Are you ready to exceed your limits? Then pick a book from the one below and start learning yet another new language. I can't imagine anything more fun, fulfilling, and exciting!

If you'd like to see the entire list of language guides (there are a ton more!), go to:

>>http://www.amazon.com/Dagny-Taggart/e/B00K54K6CS/<<

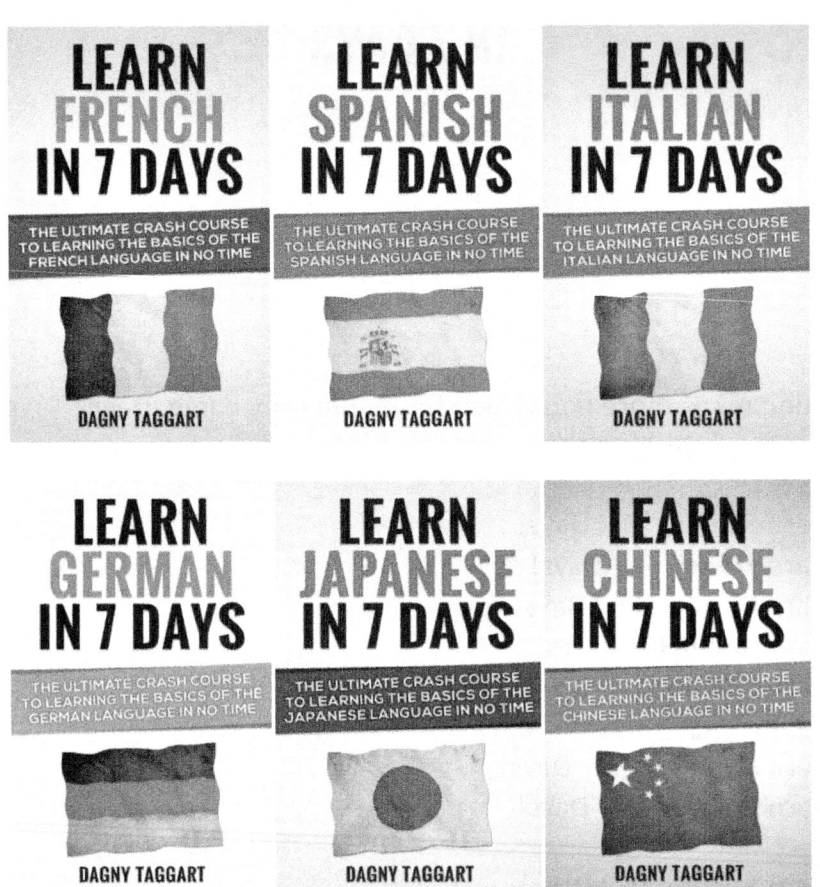

About the Author

Dagny Taggart is a language enthusiast and polyglot who travels the world, inevitably picking up more and more languages along the way.

Taggart's true passion became learning languages after she realized the incredible connections with people that it fostered. Now she just can't get enough of it. Although it's taken time, she has acquired vast knowledge on the best and fastest ways to learn languages. But the truth is, she is driven simply by her motive to build exceptional links and bonds with others.

She is inspired everyday by the individuals she meets across the globe. For her, there's simply not anything as rewarding as practicing languages with others because she gets to make friends with people from all that come from a variety of cultures. This, in turn, has broadened her mind and thinking more than she would have ever imagined it could.

Of course, as a result of her constant travels, Taggart has become an expert on planning trips and making the most of time spent out of what she calls her "base" town. She jokes that she's practically at the nomad status now, but she's more content to live that way.

She knows how to live on a manageable budget weather she's in Paris or Phnom Penh. She knows how to seek out the adventures and thrills, no doubt, lying in wait at any city she visits. She knows that reflection on each every experience is significant if she wants to grow as a traveler and student of the world's cultures.

Because of this, Taggart chooses to share her understanding of languages and travel so that others, too, can experience the same life-altering benefits she has.

CPSIA information can be obtained at www.ICGtesting.com
Printed in the USA
LVOW03s2110110515

438055LV00016B/376/P